I Am

Hagar

Kinita
Aug 2015

I Am
Hagar

Forgotten No More

Kinita Kadnar Schripsema

credo
house publishers

Contents

Introduction

Oswald Chambers writes in his book, *My Utmost for His Highest*, "The natural must be turned into spiritual by sacrifice, otherwise a tremendous divorce will be produced in the actual life . . . Abraham had to offer up Ishmael before he offered up Isaac. Some of us are trying to offer up spiritual sacrifices to God before we have sacrificed the natural. The only way in which we can offer a spiritual sacrifice to God is by presenting our bodies a living sacrifice" (December 10 entry).

My hope is that whether you are a follower of Christ or not, you will be encouraged in your story . . . we all have one!

In the story found in Genesis 16 of Abraham, Sarah, and Hagar, we read that since Sarah couldn't conceive, she brought an Egyptian slave known as Hagar to sleep with Abraham, in hopes that she would provide him with a child. They chose their own path. They didn't wait on God. When Hagar found out she was pregnant with Abraham's child and was being mistreated by Sarai, she ran to the riverside and cried out to God in hopes that he would hear her, see her and rescue her from her plight. We read that God does indeed hear her cry. In fact, the Hebrew name for God is revealed: *El Roi*, the "God who sees." That day, God heard Hagar's cry and saw her state and promised that he would "increase your descendants so much that they will be too numerous to count" (Genesis 16:9).

In Genesis 16:11 we read, "The angel of the LORD also said to her: 'You are now pregnant and you will give birth to a son. You shall name him Ishmael, for the LORD has heard of your misery.'"

Continuing on in Genesis 16:13, "She gave this name to the LORD who spoke to her: 'You are the God who sees me,' for she said, 'I have now seen the One who sees me.'"

God brought forth his promise to Abraham and Sarah and she eventually birthed a son and they named him Isaac. We read later in Genesis that Abraham was called to sacrifice his son Isaac on the altar. The LORD eventually provides for Abraham a ram in the thicket so that his son doesn't physically lose his life. This is a foreshadowing to the New Testament where we are told of the provision God made for our sin through his one and only Son Jesus Christ. He took our place on the cross and became a sacrifice for our sin.

The "natural" sacrifice Oswald Chambers talks about might be referring to Ishmael, and the "spiritual" sacrifice, as I see it, was Isaac. However, it translates well into our own lives of surrender. Ishmael was born out of a physical decision Abraham made while Isaac was the product of God's design and timing. As believers we are called to live our lives as a living sacrifice as Paul describes it in Romans 12:1–2. Until we do that, and Oswald concurs, then we cannot honestly offer up spiritual sacrifices.

I am Hagar, not because I got pregnant out of wedlock or because I can identify with being a slave girl, but because I know what it means to cry out to God about a pregnancy, child-rearing, and just growing up. I identify with her pain of disappointment when things didn't go my way. I identify with her fear of being pregnant and eventually dealing with strong-willed kids that often brought me to the edge on many occasions. Over the years, I cried out to people, and never felt like they heard me. Don't get me wrong, I'm certainly glad for their efforts, but there were many seasons where I truly felt alone and unheard. Rejected, ignored, shunned, feeling like a misfit. As I wrote this book, I grew to understand that I was more like Hagar than I realized. For years I had been a slave to people's view of me and a slave to wanting to fit in. That all changed when I began to truly understand how God was writing my story and what he desired for me as his daughter.

The person I needed was God. I needed him to hear me, to see me, to listen, and to make a way. Just like Ishmael and Isaac, God created my children and he created yours. It doesn't matter under what circumstances they were created, it just matters that you and I never forget that they were created by his hands. Knowing this gives me great peace that the God of the Universe took the time to create the children we have and entrusted them to us. Just like God chose Hagar to be the mother of Ishmael, Sarah to be the mother of Isaac, and Mary to be the mother of Jesus, he also handpicked me to be the mother of each of our four precocious children. He also handpicked you for yours. God doesn't make mistakes. Only we do.

As the mother of four children, two of whom are extremely strong-willed, I have had my share of struggle in parenting them. There were many times I cried out to God, wondering if he was hearing me. Then when I knew he was hearing me, I wondered why there were no results. Why were my prayers not being answered? I eventually learned that my prayers weren't his prayers for me. There began the journey of deep surrender and sacrificial living. Not easy, I assure you.

When our oldest turned eighteen, I found myself thinking the common thought most parents do: "I wish I knew then what I know now." The funny thing about that statement is that had I not gone through those years where God shaped my will and character and taught me how to surrender through the various struggles and trials, I would not have had the right heart for God to produce the fruit he wanted me to possess. Those experiences were ways in which he rototilled the soil in my soul, so to speak. But since this book isn't just about my experiences as a mother, I assure you that God also used my interracial marriage to shape me and to weave more of himself into my story. To our surprise it wasn't the cultural difference that caused us stress, as some people might think, but the very fact that two sinful beings decided to unite their lives and raise kids together.

So why write a book about my own story? Sounds a little narcissistic if you ask me. It is if it is all about me. But it isn't. This book is about God's faithfulness in my life. His hand in my journey. His direction and leading, empowering and blessing. It is about the fruit that he has created through the pain and struggle I experienced along the way. Hide it under a bushel—*no!* I say that not just as an extrovert who has learned she needs to process out loud but because of God's calling in my life.

He has called me to write this book. I have chosen to obey. It hasn't been easy and it has definitely taken a very long time, in my estimation.

However, every step of the way, I was being shaped, renewed, heard, and led. As a result of writing this book, I have seen the glory of the LORD shine through the darkest moments. When I wondered if I should just "throw in the towel," the Holy Spirit would gently remind me to keep going and surrounded me with friends who had my back. I thought this book was for you, my reader, but it ended up being more for me. It became my heart song to a God so great and yet so intimate. I want to share this journey with you. My journey along the riverside crying out to God.

Will you join me? My prayer is that you will not only be encouraged in your journey to finding Jesus, but that you will hear his still, small voice.

Call to him, he is waiting to hear your voice.

Life is hard, sometimes we make it that way by taking it into our own hands.

Why not put down your flesh and take up your cross and follow him?

Part 1

God Sees Me

1

Narrow Road

As I write this, I am recovering from a stent placement surgery just below my left kidney. Over the past few months I have experienced several unexplained infections and constant pain in that area. After many medical tests, it was determined that I had a small block in that area. Things weren't flowing well from my kidney to my bladder. One of the tests showed that the block was a result of a narrowing of the ureter that connected those two organs. Thus the need for a stent placement that would widen the tube, eliminate pain and produce better flow. It worked!! It also gave me the inspiration to write this.

Once again, God used an experience in my life to make a connection to my spiritual walk. My hope is that you will also be encouraged and perhaps even challenged to consider how your spiritual journey is going. Through various Scriptures and sermons on the subject, we are often being encouraged or challenged (depending on your perspective) to take the "road less traveled," to travel the narrow road, or to enter through the narrow gate to discover the life God has planned for us. Matthew 7:13–14 says, "Enter through the narrow gate. For wide is the gate and broad is the road that leads to destruction, and many enter through it. But small is the gate and narrow the road that leads to life, and only a few find it."

The physical narrowing in my body caused much pain that often needed to be medicated. Yet, I soon learned that medication was a temporary fix. This was a structural issue that required attention in a different way. Just like it took a few tests to find the narrowing in my body, I believe it takes a few (sometimes more) "tests" to find the "narrow road" that God wants us to use in our own personal journeys. Sadly, we use many temporary fixes till we make the decision to *fix* our eyes on Jesus for the duration of the journey. The potential of having pain in both of these situations is very great.

The narrowing of my ureter didn't allow toxins to be removed from my body in an efficient way. As a result, it caused much undue pain. That's how sin works too. It causes undue pain, damages us, and then eventually pours out on those around us. Sin is a toxin that needs to be removed from our souls. I quickly realized in my heart what I knew in my head, that my sin was slowing down the flow of the Holy Spirit in my life. Sin is a blocker to the work of the Holy Spirit. During this time of healing and discovery, not only did I experience physical pain postsurgery, but I was also greatly challenged in some areas of my character (which has its own pain scale). Just like I needed a doctor to help determine the cause and location of the pain, I needed the Holy Spirit to shed light on the areas in my life that weren't working according to the plan God had for me. Through confession, I discovered that I had allowed myself to believe some lies from the Enemy. Lies that were allowing him to steal, kill, and destroy my calling (John 10:10).

For the past several years I have prayed the prayer, "*Lord, help me to listen to and obey the promptings of the Holy Spirit.*" During those years I also became more aware of the sin in my life. As I confessed and repented those sins, over time I came to an understanding of how and where God was calling me to live out Matthew 7.

I have watched him strengthen some gifts, reshape others, shelve a few as he has lead me on the track I am on today. The timing of this surgery is not the least bit perplexing. God is sovereign and has every minute of my life planned out already. I trust him to carry me on this narrow road. I trust him to relieve the pain and discomfort I experience every step of the way. As I stay connected to the Vine, the Holy Spirit convicts me of my sin and refreshes me with the cleansing that comes from the blood of Christ.

He is drawing me to him and he will do the same for you.

Sin separates us from God. The death of Jesus bridges that separation and stomps out sin when we choose to believe and receive him. The abundant life (John 10:10) really is found by traveling the narrow road. That is the gift God wants us to enjoy and be blessed by.

Reflection

What temporary fixes are you using to deal with pain in your life?

What is the sin in your life that is not allowing the Holy Spirit complete access?

How and where is your narrow road?

2

Becoming A Turtle

Transformation Requires Surrender

Several years ago, I heard some fascinating and intriguing family stories that really got me thinking. Since some of the stories might bring disappointment and sadness to some family members who might be reading this, I will choose not to share them. Suffice it to say that through some of those stories I came to understand that I come from a very long line of dangerously strong women.

As I got closer to my fortieth birthday, I discovered that a turtle represented a "strong woman" in the Native American culture (of which I am not, for those who don't know that).

Right away, I knew what I wanted for my fortieth birthday . . . a tattoo of a turtle. Now that you've recovered from the shock that Kinita has a tattoo . . . like most tattoos, this one has great significance. It is a turtle with its head cocked up set at the foot of a cross. You see, God and I had a little chat and through reading Scriptures and godly counsel, it became clear that I would have to surrender some things in my life. Sounded doable. I also learned that I would need a more concrete reinforcement, thus the tattoo.

Little did I know what was going to happen over the course of the next few years.

That was a busy year. That year I learned a lot of things, sometimes simultaneously. I learned that I had a toxic strength that only a loving God would accept me with. Eventually, he would use his gentle and holy strength to mold me and shape my strengths so they would be more useful to him. After reading a book called *The High Cost of High Control* by Dr. Tim Kimmel, which led to another (secular) book called *Now, Discover Your Strengths* by Marcus Buckingham and Donald O. Clifton, PhD, the second book gave me a task to take a strengths test. On the computer, I would be required to answer several questions that would eventually "diagnose" my strengths and give me the results of my top five. For not being a lover of tests, this one was great. I walked away with a "diagnosis" that would look like this: Connectedness, Responsibility, Activator, Belief, and Winning-Others-Over (in short CRAB-WOO).

Just by themselves, they are a great list of strengths that help me develop in confidence, not only in ministry but also in parenting and my marriage as well. When I stopped and took a deeper look at each of them, it became quite clear that a couple of those strengths really required some tempering. In the Christian life, as we grow to become God-glorifying believers, Scripture teaches us to be "weak," to make less of ourselves so God can become more in and through us. There are thirty-three verses that help us unpack "weakness" in the Bible. Strengths are good for us to have. But they also have a hidden side that could cause us to develop a hard heart, or grow a belief that "we don't need others, we are strong enough by ourselves." I've learned (through several situations-gone-bad) that the best results come when we can acknowledge our weaknesses in the midst of those strengths.

Over time, it became very clear that I was having trouble managing my Responsibility and Activator strengths. Responsibility was the strength, but had the potential of presenting as Control.

Activator was a strength that was going to take a little more work to subdue. To *not* activate in a situation would require me to grow self-control (which happens to be a fruit of the Spirit). I learned that with surrendering Responsibility to the LORD and the work of the Holy Spirit, he would give me responsibilities of his choosing. By surrendering my Activator strength in the same way, it would allow God to grow self-control and patience in my life. Both of which are fruit of the Spirit that I needed in my life. (I just didn't know it.)

Let me give you an example of how that played out in my life. My firstborn broke me in by way of his stubborn, strong-willed, defiant, disobedient, and hard heart. However, I think I did what any good mother would do. I took my responsibility seriously. So seriously that the lines between what was important to discipline and what wasn't were quite blurry as he approached his teen years. As God addressed my strength of responsibility, he made it very clear that I was to surrender my son, just like Abraham brought his son, Isaac, before the LORD and laid him on the altar. No I didn't build an altar made with wood, and I didn't hold a knife over him. (However, sadly, some of the words I said over him might have looked like knives, they were so sharp.) I came to an understanding that even though I was being a responsible parent in most things, the job of my son's heart was in God's hands. So I closed my eyes and stretched out my empty hands before the LORD. I imagined that I was standing before the cross, as I sat in my living room. I envisioned my son lying across my hands as I lifted him up in surrender to God. That day *I chose to let God be God in my son's life and I would go back to being his mother.*

An Activator is a person, who lives life with the following question at the forefront of his or her mind: "When can we start?" Over the years I have been known to be impatient for action (my husband need not respond to this). Okay, so sometimes I still am . . . but right now, you are the one wondering when I'm going to make my point, right? Just saying.

In the book *Now, Discover Your Strengths* the authors put it very clearly for us Activators, by saying, "Action and thinking are not your opposites. Action is the best device for learning. You make a decision, you take action, you look at the result, and you learn. This learning informs your next action and your next. How can you grow if you have nothing to react to? Well, you believe you can't."

The next part of their explanation conflicts with my faith and belief in a sovereign God, but I'll share it anyway, so you can perhaps hear why. The authors go on to say, "You must put yourself out there. You must take the next step. It is the only way to keep your thinking fresh and informed. The bottom line is this: You know you will be judged not by what you say, not by what you think, but by what you get done. This does not frighten you. It pleases you."

If I were to write that portion of the definition from a faith perspective, it might sound something like this: "You must wait on the LORD, allowing him to show you the next step. Stay in prayer and allow the Holy Spirit to renew your mind while you wait. You know you'll be judged by what you say and also by what you think. You don't want people just to see what you get done. It frightens you to live a life that doesn't please God."

God has been gracious and very faithful in my life, every step of the way. *I am nothing without him and I mean everything to him.* Every door has been opened and closed by him. If I'm really honest, not every request has made it to the pages of my journal. Some have remained in my heart. Sometimes wondering if the request was really worth praying for or worth God's time. Yet my Sovereign God remained faithful and time and time again answered those prayers as well. However, almost always not in the way I was expecting, but in the way I needed.

For the last several weeks, I have started to feel like that turtle . . . humbled and blessed. But I know God isn't finished with me yet. I'm just celebrating his goodness. I'm okay with that. If I get too far ahead of myself, then this Activator is going to get a serious time-out!

Reflection

Do you know your strengths and weaknesses?

How do your strengths and weaknesses impact your journey of surrender?

How and when have you seen your strength become a weakness?

Where do you tend to get ahead of God?

3

The Turtle, *Not* the Hare

Slow and Steady

For those who don't know me, one of my biggest struggles is maintaining a healthy exercise schedule.

Over the years I've spent good money on the best equipment. First, a treadmill I bought on sale, justifying its use for only a couple years (or months), at which point it became a dust collector.

Then there was this abs machine that would help me do those rolling push-ups, but was gone at the next garage sale. There was the rowing machine and a glider (both the manual kind). I really knew what manual meant and that I would have to do more work and hopefully get results sooner. However, I was forgetting I would first need to get on them.

I can't forget the stair stepper that I could work out on upstairs, for convenience, and I would be able to combine it with my three-pound weights for strength training (Note: the only thing I was strengthening was my brain by making excuses as to why I wasn't using it). It would also take more than the handful of times of using it to get the buff, tight thighs and other not-so-jiggly body parts I was hoping for. The countless tapes, DVDs, and CDs didn't help in securing a healthy pattern of exercise either. Nothing seemed to work. I was finally at a point where I was willing to admit that I would need to do something, anything to get even close to the results I wanted. (I'm hoping by now you are able to relate; if not keep reading.)

I thought it was motivation I lacked. So I thought that by watching "The Biggest Loser" (a television show that followed the weight loss of various people as they did different exercises), I would grow a section in my brain that would produce that kind of motivation. I quickly realized that it was discipline I lacked, not motivation. I kept watching the show, but added a caramel sundae to the routine, instead of squats and crunches. (A bad habit once a week isn't really that bad, right?)

During that time I also signed up for e-mails from Jillian Michaels, that show's host. (Unfortunately, I was motivated to delete them every day because I couldn't keep up.) I believed that if I heard her encouragement at another time in the day, I'd do something about it. Well, it took a few years, but I did something about it. Her encouragement one significant day? "Slow and steady wins the race." Unfortunately, I kept only the title. It got my attention, because it revealed a connection to the Christian walk.

Slow and steady . . .

"Seek first his kingdom and his righteousness, and all these things will be given to you as well" (Matthew 6:33).

We could have all the resources in the world to help us get disciplined in our Christian walk (even though all we really need is the Bible). But if we never use them, it won't make a difference. I've heard that statistically the average household has four to six Bibles in it, most of which have never even been opened.

Wins the race . . .

". . . You have fought the good fight, you have finished the race" (see 2 Timothy 4:3–8). "Well done" is what I want to hear from my Savior. Not about how well I managed my exercise routine (or didn't) but by how I lived my life. That is the race I am running. Sometimes I feel very out of breath, only to realize that I am running in my own strength. Several years ago, I heard this prayer from our pastor: "*LORD, help me to listen to and then obey the prompting of Your Holy Spirit.*"

I made a commitment to say that prayer every morning and several times throughout the day. I can honestly say, I have finally found an "exercise" that fits my life well.

Reflection

How are you getting in shape spiritually?

What are you needing to do and willing to do to get in shape spiritually?

Where in your life do you need more strength or endurance and what are you doing to maintain it?

Who is God asking you to share your story with?

4

My Will: "I Don't Want to *Be*, I Want to *Do*"

(Inspired by Micah 6:8)

We live in a "doing" culture. Whether it is for ourselves, our spouses, or our children, we do. Some might even admit that they like "doing." That they like staying busy. "It makes me feel productive," "It makes me feel useful," "It makes me feel successful," we say. Unfortunately, that word also holds a negative connotation because it has been known to cause "hardworking men" to morph into "workaholics" that create an environment with potential to destroy the family. Mothers spend less and less time engaging their children or caring for themselves, perhaps because "doing" brings greater satisfaction than "being" does.

In this Western culture of ours, I believe we approach "doing" as an idol and don't even know it. We are blinded to the reality that busyness is destroying all that God has built up in humankind. We go on as if busyness is a calling and yet we don't take the time to connect with our Creator God to see what it is he created us to do. Therefore, I believe, busyness takes us away from an intimate relationship with that very God we speak of.

In his book *Counterfeit Gods*, Tim Keller suggests that we have *internal* and *external* idols. He goes on to suggest that perhaps our external busyness has a connection to a hidden, internal idol. "It is impossible to understand a culture without understanding its idols . . . but the specific answer in any actual circumstance is that there is something you feel you *must* have to be happy, something more important to your heart than God himself" (p. 166).

What do you really get from "doing" all the time and staying busy? (i.e., *staying* busy). What is it that you feel you *must* have as a result of doing? Could it be that your soul gets a deep satisfaction like nothing else you've ever experienced? Or perhaps it is about your desire to feel accomplished, successful? Maybe it is to impress friends, or better yet, the in-laws? Worse yet, you fear being still?

I believe, there are two sides of the concept of "doing." One side is "doing for the sake of doing." Staying busy.

The flip side is "doing, because God has called us to." That might look like obedience. Doing right (not to be mistaken for "being right"), as in Micah 6:8, "To act justly [right], to love mercy, and to walk humbly with your God." *Doing* God's will as it applies to your life. Living right according to what God is asking. By his ways not your own. Clothing ourselves with the righteousness of God. *Doing* life so it brings glory to God and not glory to self.

Which brings me to another word from the title. *Be.*

In order for us to do God's will we first need to make time to *be* with him. His message for us comes in the form of a love letter. The Bible. His Word is precious and he wants us to be filled with it. When we choose to *be* with God, we learn to fill ourselves with more of him. With more of his likeness. Being shaped into the person he created us to *be.*

When we are intentional about seeking him out as it says in Matthew 6:33, "Seek first his kingdom and his righteousness, and all these things will be given to you as well," we will not only learn about ordering our time but will also be immersed in his unconditional love and acceptance for us.

Sometimes it means we need to put our God-time at the top of our to-do list (so to speak), in order for us to make a habit of being in his presence.

In my experience, taking the time to be still and available to hear God's voice has allowed me to discover that he was waiting to share some deep truths with me. Sometimes ones that healed deep wounds, at other times great confirmation of his unending love for me, all the while, shaping me for his purpose.

A lifelong favorite verse of mine says it so much more clearly: "We are God's handiwork, created in Christ Jesus to do good works, which God prepared in advance for us to do" (Ephesians 2:10). With a message like that, why would I want to live my life without Jesus? I wouldn't!

In Micah 6:8 tells us to "love mercy." We are to love mercy. Not just "like" it (as a Facebook option), but "love" it. It is a command. Since mercy means not getting what you deserve. Do you love not getting what (you think) you deserve?

Mercy is not one of my strengths. I have done much to study it and understand it because it is what my LORD did for me on the cross. As I spend time being with Jesus and his Word, he is growing my understanding of the Word. I deserved death for my sin. He showed me mercy. Yes, I'd say I'm loving that. But the reality is Jesus took upon himself what was meant for me. Truly humbling.

Then at the end of the same passage, "Walk humbly with your God." It takes humility to come before such a loving, powerful, all-knowing God. We bow down, we surrender. We confess, we lean in, we hold on to. We walk. Daily. Not just in the midst of our struggles but in preparation for them. We press in. However we show up, he accepts us, receives us, loves us, and forgives us.

In John 16:33 God tells us, "I have told you these things, so that in me you may have peace. In this world you will have trouble. But take heart! I have overcome the world."

Isn't that good news that we have a God that has overcome the world? He gave his Son on our behalf (mercy). He provided a solution for our chaos (Jesus). We are called to walk *with* him in this journey called life, especially those that confess him with their mouths. But instead, we get busy with the things of the world. It's okay to love "doing," but imagine how much more you can do after you have set aside quality time to be with the God who knows how your story goes?

If you remember nothing else from this chapter, remember this: "*You were created to be a human being not a human doing.*"

Reflection

How are you being?

How and what are you doing?

What does "being busy" mean to you?

Who are you being?

What is God doing in your life?

5

Confessions of a Speeder

The other day I got pulled over for speeding (please don't judge!). It was in town. It was during the day. In fact, it was at the beginning of the day when I was getting to the first of many appointments of that day. The worst part of it, for me anyway, was that I was pulled over in front of my church. Don't worry, I hear you laughing.

Back story (i.e., my side of the story): I had a great start to my day. The sun was shining and the radio had a great driving song on. My only problem (that morning) was that *I wasn't paying attention to the speed limit signs* on that street. I honestly didn't think I needed to, since I had gone down that same street countless times in the past eleven years. Yes, I got pulled over. The officer was friendly, while I was giddy like a school girl (out of embarrassment) and all smiles. After all, I was guilty; he knew I knew it and I was going to comply. Yet, in an attempt to get out of a ticket I did what most law-abiding drivers would have done. I owned my actions and was very apologetic and respectful of the officer's position, but all the while I was making sure to smile and bat my eyelashes, just in case (i.e., my husband's side of the story). Whew, just a warning.

(Side note: The next day, my husband was in the same spot, with the same officer, for the same reason, and he got a ticket. He blames my smile and dark eyes, calling it "gender profiling." Really now? He might be right since that was not the first time for either of us.)

I'm a rule follower (although it is a challenge when it involves speed). Not just when it's good for me, but because I believe it is the right thing to do. After all, speed limit signs are black and white right? Literally and figuratively. There is no gray! So what happened that day when I got pulled over for speeding? Why didn't I follow the rule on the speed limit sign? Mind you, I'm definitely more vigilant when the children are with me in the car, especially when the permit-driver is on board. Just sayin'.

I could come up with a whole list of excuses . . . but to save your time and mine, I won't. I was speeding that day because I wasn't paying attention. *I wasn't being mindful of the warning signs around me.* I was doing my own thing. I was going at my speed instead of the speed set for me, and it was in black and white!

Sound familiar? Are you a speeder? A rule follower or rule breaker?

Well, all this reminiscing brought me to a place of contemplating the times I have gone ahead, "faster" than God. He had set a pace for me that I needed to submit to . . . to yield to . . . and I, far too often, have tried to go ahead of him. Can you relate? I have, on so many occasions, *chosen* to go ahead of him instead of wait on him. On his timing. I wanted to do my own thing at my own pace. Because on some level, I thought I knew what was better for me than God did. Looks like the Activator in me needed a little gentle reminder to get back on track.

He has posted limit signs all over the place to help me stay at a pace that fits in his plan for my life. To go at the speed he has set for me. In his Word, the Bible, through words of a trusted friend or group. Through the sermon from the pulpit at church or one downloaded through the internet. Yes, God even uses technology to get our attention! On occasion, God has even used various health issues to slow me down and keep me on track. Yet, I too am prone to wander.

Through various experiences and time spent in God's Word, I was convicted years ago, that when things didn't go *my way*, I would (subconsciously) try to get others to do it my way. I promise you, I was not being intentional when doing that. However, in that moment I had stepped outside my lane and into theirs. "Forcing them" to go at my speed. It was a painful reality that I was trying to be their "pace car" instead of encouraging them to look to God to set their pace.

After confessing and surrendering my old ways to God, he transformed them to fit his plan for my life. I can't apologize for the way I am created (with a lead foot), but I can definitely learn to *yield* toward Jesus and the sign that gives me the best direction and boundary in my life . . . the cross. It's a daily commitment, but I choose to stay in the lane created by the shadow of the cross. Where it points and lead I will go. How about you?

God loves you and has a very specific plan for your life, at a pace he has set for you. Is he your "pace car"?

Stay in *your* lane, be *your*self in the journey, and keep *your*self connected to Jesus!

Reflection

Where, in your journey, are you going ahead of or lagging behind God?

Who or what is your "pace car"?

What do you need to do different in order to stay in pace with God?

6

The Claw, I

Remember the movie *Liar, Liar* (1997), starring Jim Carey? He plays a dad/lawyer who often breaks promises to his son and clients in the work place. You are probably already envisioning him extending his arm and forming his hand in the shape of a claw in order to tease and entice his son. Mostly to make his son laugh, and not cause pain as he so often does through the many lies he tells him.

There is another claw I want to share about, the claw of "unforgiveness."

I can't remember who shared this analogy with me, but it has been one that has stuck with me over the years and through many challenging relationships and situations. Unforgiveness in our heart is like a claw with a chain. The claw pierces our heart, wraps itself around it and the chain extends all the way to another person whom we are unwilling to forgive. The piercing sometimes leads to a suffocating and debilitating feeling. As we choose to forgive the other person before the LORD, then he is the one that fills our heart with love and compassion for another and expands it. As our heart expands, the claw loses its grip and pops off. As a result, when true forgiveness happens, you become separated from the chain that binds you to that person.

I often find myself in a place where my heart hurts. I have come to learn that the pain is from that claw of unforgiveness piercing my tender heart. Why should my heart be tender? Because I am a person that believes in Jesus and have received his forgiveness that he poured out for my sin.

A situation with a family member recently exposed such a claw creeping its way to my heart. It was attempting to pierce, it was attempting to suffocate. The old me would have fought back in my own strength to remove the claw that was attempting to damage me again—unsuccessfully of course, leaving both of us with damaged hearts in the process. It would become a tug-of-war. Nothing worked. The strong emotions we both felt would eventually yank us back to face each other in yet another painful face-off.

So, "let it go," you say? Yes, I am all too familiar with the phrase. The old me struggled to "let it go." Perhaps because I was being stubborn, because I didn't know where "it" was going to go and more importantly, I believed that the other person needed to "let it go" first (i.e., apologize and seek forgiveness). Yes, I was wanting the other person to do the very thing I was not willing to do.

In the end, I wanted to do what was right. Note, I didn't say "be right." So I did the next right thing. I prayed.

Through prayer, God not only showed me that I did in fact have unforgiveness toward that person, but also helped me visualize the place I needed to let "it" go (referring to the unforgiveness). I was to leave it at the cross. At Jesus' feet. Before the throne of grace. At the altar. As a result, I have come to appreciate the word "surrender" more in my life. With God's help, the unforgiveness was turned into surrender. You see, at the cross is where it began. The cross is where "it is finished" (John 19:30).

Jesus poured out his blood on our behalf. Whether you believe it or not is not the point, it still happened because the Bible says so in Matthew 26:28 and Luke 22:20. He took upon himself what was meant for me. "It is finished" means I don't have to find solutions for my sin or anyone else's, for that matter. I need to believe, receive, and trust in his provision, his grace, his mercy, and his forgiveness of my sin.

That day, the claw didn't pierce my heart like it had in the past because I was choosing to acknowledge the blood that was protecting it like a shield. It was his shield around my heart that protected me from allowing unforgiveness to ensnare me that day.

That day, I chose to walk in forgiveness. I chose to live out my responsibility as a follower of Christ and to be a loving parent by forgiving my child before the LORD.

Reflection

Have you received the forgiveness God has for you?

What does forgiveness mean to you?

How do you respond when you are asked to forgive someone?

What is the challenge you face when it comes to forgiving someone?

Who do you need to forgive?

What are the "claws" in your life? (For example, jealousy, pride, etc.)

7

Tekea: My Angel on the Journey

Every now and then we get tired and worn out on our journeys. But because God is a loving, caring, and providing God, he sees us and provides someone on our paths to encourage us to keep going. He does that for all of us.

"I did it, I did it!" I sang to myself as I achieved a goal to "get back on my bike." Here's the back story.

To save on gas, since prices are ridiculously high, I decided to ride my bike the eight-mile round trip to our credit union. Given my recent discovery of fear when riding alone, I mustered up the courage to push through it. This was not going to be an easy attempt. I'll admit, it wasn't as difficult as last week, so I celebrate my progress . . . thus the "I did it."

Before heading out, I called several friends to see if they would be available to join me on the bike ride. For fitness, company, and secretly I needed some moral support because I really didn't think I could do it by myself. In discovering that nobody I called was available to join me, my anxiety began to go up and also because I realized I didn't want to do this alone. So I prayed, *"God, help me take this road in your strength. I trust you. Amen."*

I headed out with a confidence and assurance that everything would be okay. I need to travel along a main road before I get to the actual trail. I was fine riding there because cars were going by and I was convinced they were cheering for me. (Probably because that's what I do when I see a biker, I cheer for them when I drive by.) I wasn't alone.

The weather was cloudy, so as I entered at the opening of the trail, it appeared darker than usual. I then began to notice the lump in my throat. Before I knew it, my eyes were burning and the tears started to flow. I was still peddling. I tried to convince myself that this wasn't about past experiences or the fact that the darkness reminded me of my loneliness, my eyes were just watering . . . "Whatever!" (said with strong sarcasm). Along the path I biked, randomly people would go by either on bike or on foot. We would exchange greetings with a smile or a small wave. But I would be sure to wipe away the tears before they would see them. It was still quite dark along the path. There is a break in the path that requires me to go up onto a main road and cross at the light. As I crossed, I heard a still small voice. *"You needed to persevere as you went through the darkness, but when you turn the corner, you'll see the Light."* I wasn't alone. He was with me. God was with me . . . just like he promised. He would never leave me . . . just like he promised. He will always make a way for me . . . just like he promised.

So I arrived at the credit union. Clearly my sweaty, out-of-breath self gave away the fact that I just came on my bike again. (The teller remembered me from the last time . . . she cheered me on.) I got back on my bike and headed home. So I did it . . . I could go further now, right? Wrong. I debated about taking the main road home with all its steep hills. Possibly stopping at the bike shop to check on a helmet that might work and see if I could get a tune-up for my bike. I also convinced myself I would have the positive support of my fellow travelers in their cars. Crazy, eh?

I heard that still small voice again. *"You've done enough for today. You need to go back the way you came."* I was almost ready for a rebellious response full of pride that might have sounded like this: *"I can do it, everyone will be proud that I went the extra mile, I have to push past this fear so by riding the steep hills I'll be able to prove that I am an overcomer."* What happened next was completely an act of God. I felt my bike veer to the right toward the path . . . I had no words.

I do believe I was being led by God on this journey . . . literally!

I came back on the same path. This time things seemed brighter. Some would say, "It's because the sun finally came out." They wouldn't be wrong. It did. But a few moments later I saw the Son come out. There was a woman on the path who had greeted me on my journey to the credit union. This time she was walking by herself. As I passed her and greeted her, she shouted something to me. I couldn't hear, so I stopped and waited for her to catch up. Her name is Tekea. She's from another country that I am familiar with for various reasons. Her accent was very strong so I strained to hear what she was trying to say. She told me she was proud of me . . . unusual affirmation from a stranger. As we talked for a few minutes, we learned that we had the same Protestant faith. She lit up and told me how much she loves God and needs him every day of her life; she wasn't a stranger at all . . . she was a Jesus-lover. The lump came back in my throat. She apologized for stopping me in my "work." (How would she know what "work" I was doing on my bike or in my soul?) The tears flowed as I thanked her for being an answer to prayer. I told her how God used her to remind me that Jesus really was on this journey with me.

The rest of our few minutes don't really matter, except that I knew, without a shadow of doubt that God provided an angel on my journey for the loneliness I was feeling today. He used a simple little bike ride to show himself to me. He took me along a path, helped me turn a corner and see the Light and gave me the strength to revisit that path, on which he already planted one of his children to affirm me to finish strong. I still need a tune-up on my bike, but the tune-up I got for my soul today will stay with me forever.

My prayer is that you would be able to take the time today (even if it's just five minutes) and ask Jesus to reveal himself to you.

Reflection

Who do you best identify with in my story?

When have you seen God's perfect timing of planting you in someone else's journey or having someone planted in yours?

Where do you need God to show himself in your journey?

What emotions do you experience when you revisit an old place in your life's journey?

8

The Open Door

(Inspired by Acts 14:1−7)

Its has often been said, "When one door closes, another one opens." While others say, "when one door closes, a window opens." So what happens when a door opens? Does one instinctively go through it? Is one cautious and pensive, all the while staring in doubt that the door is actually open?

Are there particular feelings that come when you walk through that door? Is there joy? Trepidation? A sense of freedom? A sense of accomplishment? Is it really about the door or about the One who opened it in the first place?

Journey with me, won't you? I've gone through many doors in the past four-plus decades. Some because I shoved them open—in which case things didn't end well. Some doors were opened as a result of a particular season of life I was in. I stood in front of some doors hoping and praying they would open at any moment (i.e., *my* timing). Some doors opened right in front of my eyes and I didn't see them right away, possibly because it was a door I wouldn't have picked. I learned to trust in God's timing. I learned to listen to, and then obey, how and where the Holy Spirit was leading me. Unfortunately I would still wonder to myself, "Was this door opened by God, or not?"

You see, I understand that God is Sovereign in my life. He loves me; I matter to him. I'm passionate about a deep intimate relationship with him. So I choose to sit as his feet and glean from every Word he pours out from his Book, the Holy Bible. That is the first door I open each day. I take a step into an intimate relationship with Jesus every time I open it. It is a door that opens me up to a world that, by some, is quickly forgotten between Sundays. From Genesis to Revelation—the creation, the fall, the redemption through Jesus Christ, and God's ongoing restorative work. It's all in there, behind the door, inside the covers of the Great Book. It's there where I find the answers to the many questions that brew in my heart along the way. I choose to walk through that door because I want to grow to be more like him. A few decades ago, when I was a teenage girl, I heard Jesus knocking on the door of my heart. I answered and let him in to have control over my life. Since then he has shown me door after door after door hidden in the stories that fill his Book. The possibilities have been endless.

God has a plan for you. Jeremiah 29:11–13 says, "'For I know the plans I have for you,' declares the LORD, 'plans to prosper you and not to harm you, plans to give you hope and a future. Then you will call on me and come and pray to me, and I will listen to you. You will seek me and find me when you seek me with all your heart.'"

I don't know if you see it, but there are a lot of "doors" in that passage alone. Hope. Future. Prayer. All with the promise of *finding God!*

Many people have asked me how I got to be where I am in my life. (As much as I sense a compliment in that question, I just believe I am on my journey . . . not anyone else's.) Many have also said, "they could never hear the LORD the way I do." Again, sensing another compliment, but left thinking that *everyone* who professes to be a follower of Christ *can* have such an intimate relationship with him, I know I am *not* unique.

Years ago, a mentor shared a guideline that she followed. The acronym is FAT.

F stands for *faithful*. Staying the course. Putting one foot in front of the other. Doing as you should even when you don't feel like it. Thankfully, we serve a God who will always be faithful. We need not worry about his end of the deal.

A stands for *available*. Having margin in your life. Unlike the days where our schedules are so full that if a feather fell on our heads we'd collapse. Making room on your full plate. What are the things you are carrying that you don't need to? Often we pray to receive from God what we think we want or need and we wonder why we aren't getting it. Maybe there is no room in our hands. Perhaps you're doing work that someone else is capable of doing or responsible for? (Hey, busy moms, several women have shared lately that they find it hard to get through the many tasks of the day. My questions to them have been, "Can the kids help out with age-appropriate tasks so you can find some extra minutes in your day to do what God has laid on your heart or simply get time to take care of yourself?" "How does 'doing for them' what they can do themselves impact their growth?")

T stands for *teachable*. How open is your heart to learn new things? Perhaps learning old things in a new way. What is it that God wants you to learn through the situations that touch your life? Are you willing to surrender what you need to in order to be who God wants you to be?

As I shared this with a friend recently, she responded with the following. "We know we are not FAT when we let our EGO get in the way." She then told me what EGO stood for. EGO = Edging God Out. Yikes . . . definitely *not* the way I want to live my life.

Reflection

Has God been knocking on the door of your heart? Will you answer him?

What gets in the way of taking care of yourself or allowing you to be more available for what God wants of you?

When was the last time you picked up the Bible and spent some time discovering Jesus?

Will this be the year you go through a door to become faithful, available, and teachable, or will you let your ego get in the way?

9

Food for Thought

Food inspires me. Cooking it, watching someone cooking it, and just simply eating it! I love food.

Currently, in Michigan, we are coming to the end of a season full of fun summer foods. Fresh fruits and vegetables, lots of grilled foods, potlucks and picnics filled with a variety of dishes to sink our teeth into. I enjoyed food so much this summer that I was inspired to start a picture file of some of the dishes I made.

Then it happened. God used food to speak to me. Chicken. Not cooked but raw. It happened one day when I had grilled chicken on the dinner menu. I was going to marinate it with a spicy chicken masala for those carrying adventurous taste buds, myself included, while doing a mild barbecue sauce for the less daring in the family. I chose chicken breasts and filleted them so they would grill faster and we would have more pieces to stretch the meal. Yes, I'm frugal too!

What came next, I wasn't ready for. As I filleted the chicken, I felt a lump in my throat and tears filled my eyes. No, I'm not a vegan (no offense to my vegan friends). I like meat. This was not a "sad moment for chickens" thing. But, to be honest, I didn't know what it was. I had filleted chicken breasts many times over the years, so why tears? Why now?

When I laid the first filleted chicken breast into the marinade, it was in the shape of a heart. Truth be told, I did not know that was going to happen either.

Here's what God showed me as I journaled on the experience later that night.

A chicken breast filleted does in fact take the shape of a heart. Just like a chef prepares, marinates, seasons the chicken for cooking, *the LORD does the same with our hearts*. He cuts into our hearts with his Word and encourages us to marinate in it until we are ready for what he has in store for us. His plan, his calling.

Sometimes the "marinade" might look like a long, painful life experience which we have often referred to as a "valley" in our personal journeys. The longer the meat soaks in a marinade, the better the taste and more tender the dish. *The deeper the valley, the greater the lessons for our lives.* God prepares us just the way he wants so we are ready to be "served" for his calling. If and when we submit to his authority as "Master Chef," that painful life experience doesn't necessarily become easier. Instead we might grow in our trust of God. Or God gets bigger than the pain.

I believe he also blesses us through a sweet aroma of spices that give great contentment and pleasure. Imagine yourself coming in after a long day's work and your favorite dish is being crafted just the way you like it. Your palate is being enticed before you even enter the room. It's still not as good as the first bite, but you already know how content you will be and what pleasure you will experience when you do get to taste it. That is how it is with God. He prepares a plan for us so that we can, in fact, "taste and see that the LORD is good" (Psalm 34:8).

When we first step into the plan, we are unsure and yet enticed by his hand. But we quickly find ourselves experiencing what we might call a "mountaintop" experience in our lives. When things are great and we are feeling full and perhaps even overflowing with his goodness.

Some "marinades" are rich in spices while others call for a sprinkling of sorts. Throughout our lives, God uses his Word and whatever else to sprinkle varying amounts of the fruit of his Spirit— joy, peace, patience, kindness, goodness, faithfulness, gentleness, and self-control, to prepare us for the work in a place that he has prepared in advance for us (Ephesians 2:8–10). When the right amounts of those come together, then we are ready for the next step. *He chooses the ingredients in carefully measured portions so we can carry out his call on our lives.*

Do we allow him to do that? Are we choosing to be still long enough to allow him that kind of access to our hearts? Are we resting in the "marinade" of God's "ingredients" for our lives, or are we making up our own recipe as we go? At the beginning of the summer I read a great book called *Tattoos on the Heart* by Father Gregory Boyle. Throughout the summer the LORD did open-heart surgery on me. Sometimes the pain was unbearable and I was distracted from seeking his medicine. Other times I was truly able to rest in his presence and heal. Now, at the end of this summer, I can say that I now have "tattoos on *my* heart" by the Author and Perfecter of my faith.

Did you know that God is the Master Chef who has a plan for you to avoid Hell's Kitchen?

Reflection

What is your heart marinating in?

What ingredients has God sprinkled into your story to make you who you are?

What is God preparing you for?

10

Posture

What is posture? Webster's dictionary explains it as "a body position, an attitude of the mind, an official stand or position." So I'm understanding that posture has physical and mental characteristics. That's good because I like options. So about posture . . . during the recovery period of a stent placement procedure into my ureter (a channel that connects the kidney and the bladder), I discovered something about my preferences for posture. It was uncomfortable, and I experienced great pain when sitting in a chair. The pressure I was feeling to my left side while in that posture was often unbearable. So I needed to recline. Anywhere from a forty-five degree angle to lying flat. That brought relief. It not only helped the bladder spasms to settle down but I was also able to rest.

I also discovered that I have a bad habit of slouching when sitting. Slouching was adding pain to an already sore back and wasn't doing anything to add to presentation. It probably suggested that I had a "slacker" attitude. Which I don't, but apparently what I show on the outside reflects what's on the inside. Maybe that's why my mother was always telling me to "sit up straight" when I was a child.

All these physical references to posture remind me of the postures we show through prayer. If we kneel, bow, sit, or even lay prostrate, I believe each of those show, physically, varying degrees of submission and it is always the Holy Spirit that moves us to there. The question remains, what is going on in our hearts?

During my recovery I was asked to speak at a prayer conference. Since I didn't have any activity restrictions, I accepted. What a privilege and an honor, with fun and ironic timing. To engage in a time of teaching and encouraging others in their own personal prayer walks when God was challenging and affirming me in the posture of my heart. I believe God had opened that door, and so I made the choice to walk through it. I relished in my sweet spot that day. I thoroughly enjoyed the posture the LORD granted me through that experience. As I sat in his hand, he carried me amidst the pain and discomfort I physically experienced.

This word "posture" became something I could tangibly feel. Physically, it would sometimes cause pain, while other times repositioning my body, changing my posture, would bring relief.

Here's where the second part of Webster's definition comes in. That posture is an attitude of the mind. In my experience, it is easier to change the physical one rather than the attitude of the heart. But in the end, the attitudes of our hearts are the postures that will keep.

I have a posture in my mind that I use often. It is that of surrender. Submission . . . to God.

I face the cross in my mind. I kneel at his feet in my heart. I open my hands before him to receive what he has for me. This posture is the only one that keeps me strong. Keeps me healthy. Keeps me growing forward and gives me rest at the same time. Some have called it prayer. I agree, it is. But I believe it is a lot more. This posture reminds me that I am not God and helps me acknowledge my position as his child. It is humbling.

You should try it sometime. It might be scary at first, but it will be freeing at best! Whether the medical procedure fixed my ureter permanently is up for debate. However, I believe that the work God did in my heart to reposition my posture definitely did fix my heart!

We are so often tied to God's *plan* for our lives and forget to be tied *to God!* We allow our circumstances to determine our God. Instead of allowing God to impact our circumstances.

Reflection

What is your posture?

What is preventing you from learning to do something that is better for you?

What helps or hinders you from leaning into God?

11

Deep Cries Out

Went to a four-day-long prayer conference recently. I went reluctantly. Don't get me wrong, I love prayer, I love Jesus, I love engaging both of those in community. I just didn't want to "fill my head" with more information. Stuff. However, God had much in store for me in the coming days . . . I was blown away!

On the morning of departure, during my time of Bible reading, the LORD brought me to a very powerful verse I had never read or seen before—Exodus 23:20–22. It says, "See, I am sending an angel ahead of you to guard you along the way and to bring you to the place I have prepared. Pay attention to him and listen to what he says. Do not rebel against him; he will not forgive your rebellion, since my Name is in him. If you listen carefully to what he says and do all that I say, I will be an enemy to your enemies and will oppose those who oppose you."

This prayer conference was set up so we could learn to acknowledge, embrace, and eventually dance with the third person in the Trinity, the Holy Spirit. Not at all a new concept for me. I chose to camp on that particular verse over the course of the four days to help me grow in expectancy of what the LORD was going to do. I figured that since he led me to that passage, he had a very specific plan for how it would unfold in my journey. Ironically, it became not only a time of emptying myself, but a filling of another kind. From the dynamic worship to the biblical teachings—all while dancing with the Holy Spirit—there was produced in me a filling that I find very hard to put into words. But I will try.

I learned, more intimately, how to dance with the Holy Spirit in the ways that I have been wired—to go to the places (near and far) where God is calling me. I really thought I was to focus on my upcoming trip to India and Nepal. Once again, I was wrong. Imagine that! But I (perhaps as some form of rebellion of wanting answers my way) continued to focus hard on connections being made and watched how they connected me to the speaking I would do to a culture group of women on the other side of the globe. As time went on and I was being lead by the Holy Spirit in my own personal dance, I began to see how God was gently moving my focus off the trip and onto my heart. We had some heart business to take care of. Fear, doubt, unforgiveness—my "deep" began to cry out.

I needed healing. But first I would need to open up my heart before the LORD.

Just like that song says, "we bow down, we lay our crowns, at the feet of Jesus."

My hands were full of my stuff. God was asking me to empty them. My heart was full of fear, doubt, and unforgiveness. God was asking me to confess and surrender. So I did.

Then it happened . . .

That "place" he prepared for me to be in. On the last morning of the conference we had been praying corporately for the healing of various congregations. Exposing and confessing the obstacles that were interfering with the beautifully choreographed dance the Holy Spirit was desiring to have with the local church. Generation groups were represented and prayed over and blessed. Then the LORD said to me, "*the multiethnic/multicultural church is not being represented up there and you need to say something.*" I thought I was going to pass out! So I quickly told God he must be mistaken (don't judge, please!).

Since he is *never* mistaken, he simply and gently repeated what he said. I was paralyzed in my seat. I was being asked to take a stand for those of us that have (over the generations of the organized church) been marginalized, not included, not accepted, perhaps even blatantly rejected. This made me think of Hagar, a marginalized Egyptian slave girl who needed God to rescue her.

This was no small task. I was going to have to bring the sin of racism within the church to the attention of the three (very tall and intimidating) white men in charge, in hopes that they would receive what I believe the LORD had impressed upon me. (Even now, I'm shaking at the thought of that moment.) So I prayed, I shared my thoughts with two other Jesus lovers and truth tellers, in hopes that they would support my fears. They didn't. Instead they nudged me on to the "dance floor." I was scared. Slowly and gently, the LORD began to show me that the four days of this conference was going to culminate into this one moment. If only I would take the step and go forward. They were teaching us to listen for the Holy Spirit, address obstacles, obey what the Holy Spirit was telling us, step into the situation we were being called to, confirm what the LORD was telling us through Scripture and other believers. These are things I have practiced faithfully for the past several years and yet somehow this particular moment seemed absolutely overwhelming.

Well, I did it. I took the step and approached the leaders in charge. I shared with them what the LORD had laid on my heart. I wondered if Esther (from the Bible story) had some of the emotions I was having at that moment. She too was called "for such a time as this." I received pushback from one of them, but as I submitted to the LORD's leading, he gave me a confidence to gently but firmly repeat what I had just said. As I affirmed their leadership, I knew without a shadow of doubt my heart was really submitting to the leadership of the Holy Spirit in my life.

They came to me a few minutes later and asked that I would be the voice for my sisters and brothers that have also been marginalized, ignored, and rejected. I took the opportunity to speak out for those of us who have experienced such pain in the church. As a result, several people came forward with words of confession, repentance, seeking forgiveness for themselves and on behalf of those who oppressed various groups of people. What healing, what peace, what freedom.

It doesn't mean our hard work is over as far as racial reconciliation goes, but that day God used me to stand in the gap for all those I described in the midst of generations of Christ followers. To bask in the freedom that comes from forgiveness . . . is really just a glimpse of the peace that passes all understanding. Before leaving that day, a woman who had been marginalized for several roles in her life spoke up and said she was initially ready to leave yet another Christian event that wasn't addressing the need for racial reconciliation . . . but the Holy Spirit moved her to wait. She was so glad she did. So am I.

Wow! Go God!

I don't even want to imagine what it would be like if I hadn't done the work to confess my fear, doubt, and unforgiveness.

I want to sign off with a quote from the event.

"In our dance of cooperation with the Holy Spirit, he is the director of the whole process: he calls us into the dance, leads the steps and directs our movement toward his purpose. At the same time he leaves room for our full, responsive, joyful participation.

Reflection

Where is the Holy Spirit calling you to dance? How will you respond?

What is your deep soul cry?

What is your heart/soul longing for God to answer?

Part 2

God Sees Them

12

Tug of War

The Day I Let Go of My Daughter

So it's been about four years since the adoption. The cards are packed away, the streamers are taken down along with the posters of her joining our "forever family." The excitement from friends seems long past, everyone has moved on. Except for us—it all seems so fresh yet. When will it feel like "normal"? Then again, who defined "normal"? What does it really mean anyway?

In our first year together there were frequent moments of struggle. Not the simple kind of a response of no following a request. The no was usually followed by a dark look in the eyes and body language that I was unfamiliar with. Add to that a particular tone and before I knew it, we were into a full-on struggle. Sometimes it even got physical, as I tried to calm her down.

Other times it was so verbal that I was spitting with every word. Very embarrassing to admit, and yet knowing I am not alone in this. After it was over, I was usually shaking, she was crying and trying to cool off in her room as I was pacing at the other end of the house trying to calm my racing heart down. I was experiencing a myriad of emotions, from anger at myself and at those who walked out on us to frustration with her to fear of what could happen if I did give in to the flesh completely. My need for God's power was ever so evident. After confessing the excruciatingly painful experience to God and apologizing to my daughter, I would confess my struggle to my husband. I described it in metaphorical terms. "Honey, I felt like I was wrangling a horse." This girl was and is strong both physically and with her will. These challenging situations reminded me of the truth in Ephesians 6:12, "For our struggle is not against flesh and blood, but against the rulers, against the authorities, against the powers of this dark world and against the spiritual forces of evil in the heavenly realms." I wasn't wrangling my daughter as much as it was a battle for her heart and soul and another opportunity for me to fail.

As time went on, things started to settle down. I spent more time learning about how God made me, what his call on my life was all about and then asking him to show me what he wanted for my relationship with my daughter. As a result, with each episode I became less reactive and more responsive. Surprisingly, the episodes became further and further apart. I was trusting God for her healing as I begged him to supply me with the strength and tenacity it was going to take to come alongside her in her journey. I was beginning to let go . . . of the rope that stretched from my will to hers. Little did I realize (right away anyway) that the healing was beginning deep in my soul as well.

Over the years I have come to discover the tension I live with every day between being a strong and surrendered woman versus a strong and un-surrendered woman. It exposed a real need for a sincere and consistently growing relationship with Jesus. That's probably why defiance and a lack of submission to authority make the hair on the back of my neck stand straight out. Throughout the generations in my family (possibly on both sides) there have been significant women who were very strong-willed. During this time in my life, God showed me a connection between my heritage of strong and unsurrendered women and this little girl whom we adopted. She did not want to submit. She wanted to fight for what she believed was right. I couldn't blame her, some of that was simply protective behavior she embodied as a response to what she experienced through loss and relinquishment from the early childhood years. It's not completely wrong to want to fight for what one believes in, but if there isn't first a desire to submit to an authority first, then you will always have a fight on your hands. All this reminded me of a prayer I prayed before the adoption was final—*"LORD, help me to see your thumbprint along this road we are going to travel."*

So today was one of those explosive days. Although this time, she was being passive with it and I was fighting tooth and nail (appearing aggressive) to not give in. I held my ground (tried not to raise my voice). Stayed consistent and clear (or so I thought). As the minutes went by in the day, the tension grew. We were preparing to head to a friend's house for dinner.

Then it happened. She was arguing about something and I held my position. She argued again, this time with a good dose of whining and attitude. I reacted and yet was trying to stand my ground . . . this went on longer than it should have. Finally, she made a statement that was untrue and a little ridiculous, I thought. At which point I calmly just agreed with her. I motioned her to her seat in the van and I waited. She came unglued. Screaming and kicking and crying . . . not pretty . . . a mess.

As we drove to where we were going, a light bulb went on in my head. "I let go . . ." I looked at my husband, astonished, and repeated, "I let go . . ." By now he was wondering if I had been talking to him and he had tuned out. "What do you mean?" he asked. "I let go of the rope." (Poor guy gets to play twenty questions, I'm semi-shocked.) "I was 'playing' tug-of-war with her and I let go and she fell in the mud . . . she was a mess." I found myself massaging my palms as though I felt the burn marks from an imaginary rope. I was playing tug-of-war. My will against hers. She didn't need me in the middle of the battle, she needed me to be at the finish line to let her know everything was okay, and she was okay, that the battle was over. I let go. That day I felt the rope slip out of my hand. My spirit quieted and surrendered to know that "fixing that stuff" in her wasn't my job. God has entrusted this little girl to my husband and me. He knows what is broken in her. He knows how to fix it. He even has a plan to fix it, whether here on earth or someday in heaven. He knows what's broken in all of us. It is not my job to fix what is broken in her. It is my job to come alongside her, cheer her on, and let her know when it's safe again. I can't say I'm there yet, but I've let go. I'm trusting God for the rest. For the next steps.

Today I let go and trusted my daughter into the mighty hand of God. I have chosen to surrender to him for *all* things about her. Not just when things go right. But when she feels like things are out of control, instead of getting out of control with her, I choose to provide stability and peace, the Shalom and the Shiloh with God's help. Incidentally, four years ago I was on another personal journey to surrender one of my other children because of the challenge and toxicity that came packaged in that relationship. Today, he is a new person. Today I did the same for my daughter. Today I am a new person.

Reflection

How about you, what/who has God put in your life that he is asking you to surrender?

How are you responding?

Are you caught up in the tug-of-war?

What are you fighting with God about?

My prayer is that you would share your "tug-of-war" story with a trusted, truth-telling friend. Allow that person to walk with you in your journey. Who knows, maybe they are the solution for you to get more intimate with Jesus.

13

Loss or Gain

Our daughter is adopted from local foster care here in our city. The very fact that we had the privilege to adopt her means she had to experience a permanent loss that she might grieve throughout her life. On the one hand, even though we see adoption as a "gain" for us, in her mind, and in the minds and hearts of most adoptees, it is primarily about the "loss." In a sense, their pain is our gain. Yet so often adoptive families approach the whole thing from an adoption standpoint without acknowledging the loss the child has experienced and perhaps how deeply they have been affected.

This loss, as they perceive it, begins to be the filter by which they approach every situation in their lives.

Adoption is a beautiful relationship, but for the child(ren) it can be a painful reminder of the loss of a relationship that began in the womb. Whether they "knew" their birth mothers or not, the reality is that attachment begins in the womb. As in our case, where a child is adopted after the age of three, considering it an "older child adoption," the child has to learn a new attachment when the original one was created for him, especially if he has any kind of memory of his past. They need to navigate waters that are very foreign to them and also ones they didn't choose, forcing them to frequently uncover the pain of that loss. Control of situations, relationships, and their surroundings becomes very integral to these wounded children, sometimes unknowingly, which makes the healing journey that much more difficult.

After the "adoption honeymoon" came to an end, I realized that I needed to be a better student of our daughter. I paid close attention to patterns that sent her into negative behaviors and to situations that caused her great anxiety. I watched her interact with her peers and friends that we would socialize with, praying every step of the way that God would give me eyes to see her and not just her behaviors. There were many frustrations for her and for me along the way and I found myself often crying out to God in agony over her pain and also in my need for help.

I am a firm believer that there is not a one-size-fits-all solution when it comes to parenting. For me, parenting a girl was already presenting itself as a great challenge, so I needed to be very clear about her adoption pain so I could help her navigate the healing journey in her life.

Seeking God was my time to surrender my will to him and to be intimately involved with his plan for her. After all, he is writing her story and knowing that he chose me to be her adoptive parent, although frustrating at times, gave me great hope that he had a specific plan for her life that required my wiring.

I learned often that this wiring of mine would need to be completely submitted to his authority first, in every area.

Surrender is a challenging journey for sure. However, I am on a short list of people in my life who actually enjoy it. It has taught me to think less of myself and more about God. It has been so freeing to know that I can take the challenging situation and place it in the hands of God for his purposes. Over time, I have realized it is actually easier to surrender her and submit to God's way than it is to give in to the frustrations and challenges I have faced along the way as an adoptive parent.

Surrendering is a constant dying to self. It is losing myself so that I might gain more of Christ. Five years ago when we first adopted our daughter, my prayer was that God would show me his thumbprint every step of the way. I just didn't realize, at the time, that it would take this much surrendering to make that happen. Yes, he also had to deal with some pride along the way.

Looks like our daughter and I have something in common. We are both learning to appreciate loss and gain in our story.

Reflection

What have you lost and are now grieving?

How has God shown up in your story?

What has God used in your life to teach you surrender?

14

Mountaintops

I love to hear about "mountaintop" experiences. They just give such joy, hope and encouragement for those of us that hear them or experience them ourselves. For instance, in 2012 I took a trip to Mussoorie, India, which is located at the foothills of the Himalayan mountains. From every angle on any one of those mountain ranges, the view was breathtaking. On a clear day, every mountaintop had a clear view of another. There is an old familiar Carpenters' song lyric that came to mind as I looked over the edge of the cliffs: "I'm on the top of the world looking down on creation." It made me wonder if God sits in heaven and says that from time to time.

Another mountaintop experience I recently had was that of watching our son graduate from the Michigan Youth Challenge Academy, a military school that invests in the lives of young people to help them find their way in life. I was elated and extremely proud of the work he did to graduate with a corporal title in front of his name. Months ago we were at a crossroad with our teenage son. His defiance was off the charts and so was our inability to work things out rationally. We had done everything we knew to do to help our son break free. We had also been trusting God, surrendering our son, and praying faithfully for God to make a way and lead us to a solution. He did. Not in a way that was conventional or expected. But it didn't matter; we trusted God and he came through for us.

There are some other mountaintop experiences, however, that are nothing like one would expect. Filled with anxiety, fear, nervousness, wonder, and questions. Abraham was on such a mountain when he was called by God to sacrifice his son on an altar. I wonder how Abraham felt as he obeyed what God was calling him to do. *Was he feeling anxious in the midst of that obedience? Did he think that he had a choice between faith and flesh?* I know I trusted God for our son, but I was so beaten up emotionally as his mother. I was desperate for a solution, maybe a little different than Abraham, but I knew we were still being led by God.

My struggle with faith and flesh stems from my childhood. I was a strong-willed child myself, or so "they" say. But as I entered adulthood, I began to understand God's desire and my need to surrender, and I wanted my life to be completely surrendered to Jesus Christ, every step of the way. I wonder what kind of emotions Abraham and his son Isaac experienced on top of that mountain? In the end, the LORD provided a ram in the thicket, before the knife would touch the boy. I'm thinking that Isaac must have been elated! Free! Thankful! Generations later, Jesus Christ became the ultimate sacrifice, God's solution for our sin on a cross—ironically on that very same mountain.

When our son came home, I was elated, thankful—my son was free! He had come home with a softer heart—with *all* his isms in tow. God had also done some amazing healing in me during his absence. Although, at the time of this writing, our relationship with our son is not yet completely restored, we have grown in our trust and surrender to God. From time to time, I still struggle to apply faith over flesh, but I am getting better at it with God's help. Through the years of our journey, my confidence in God has grown. I have

seen the hand of God in the life of my son and our family. I choose
to trust him for what is next for our son, for all our children.

During this past Christmas season the one song that brought
tears to my eyes was "Go Tell It on the Mountain." At first I didn't
know why. Then the LORD showed me the connection. He has called
me to do just that, to share the message of hope with others. If I
choose flesh over faith, I won't be able to answer his call on my life.
So for me, it continues to be a daily reminder of my need for Jesus.
I choose faith over flesh so that I can truly experience his power in
action when I "Go Tell It on the Mountain."

Isaiah 30:17 says, ". . . till you are left like a flagstaff on a
mountaintop, like a banner on a hill."

Faith or flesh . . . which will you choose? The next time you
find yourself on a mountaintop or even in a valley looking at a
potential mountain, don't only thank God for the great time you
are having, ask him to show you if there is anything else that needs
surrendering while your heart is so open and filled with joy. If you
are in a valley right now, surrender and have faith—God *will* come
through for you. Let him be your solution today.

Reflection

Will you go and tell it on a mountaintop that Jesus Christ is born?

Is he your provider?

Or are you perhaps a person who feels stuck in a valley and just needs the comfort and presence of the Savior all to yourself right now?

What is stopping you from have the abundant life? (John 10:10).

Isaiah 30:21 says, "This is the way; walk in it." In John 14:6 Jesus says, "I am *the* way and *the* truth and *the* life" (italics mine). Submit, surrender, walk, have faith . . . *go with God!*

15

Daddy, Can You Help Me?

As I sit here watching my husband play at the park with the kids, he is in his element. Right now he is playing with Anna. She wants to swing on the monkey bars. She loves the monkey bars. She tries and tries to jump up and reach them but after several tries is unsuccessful; then she says, "Daddy, can you help me?" So Ken with one strong arm picks her up so she can reach. Then off she goes across the bars.

This goes on for many minutes. She tries, unsuccessfully, and says again, "Daddy, can you help me?" He helps her over and over. After a while Ken goes on to play with the others. She doesn't see him walk away; then she screams, "Daddy! Daddy!" Sadly she leans up against the pole until she sees her daddy come back to help. Cheering her along each bar. He guides and protects her through the challenge. We cry out, "Abba Father." "Daddy, are you there?"

I find myself doing this a lot as a parent of a daughter. I had what I call "on-the-job training." I have come to learn a deep dependence on God in this area. I didn't seek him as much or enough while the other children were little. If I did, it wasn't with as much passion or vigor. Funny thing is, I wasn't so much wondering whether or not God was present; I knew he would be. He called me to this kind of parenting. He trusted me with this prepackaged, brown-eyed beauty. He was never going to leave me out on a limb. He would always go right out there with me. He knew what she needed. He knew what I needed to be the parent that would see her to the finish line of childhood. Yes, there were days when I felt overwhelmed, but with his help I survived and even thrived.

My cry was often, "Daddy, can you help me?" I couldn't parent her on my own. I knew I needed him. I had learned that her adoption wasn't about what we gained but about what she lost. I was going to need the presence of Jesus every step of the way.

Proverbs 3:5–6 says, "Trust in the LORD with all you heart and *lean not on your own understanding*; in all your ways submit to him, and he will make your paths straight" (italics mine). As much as I had a good understanding of parenting before she joined our family, I knew it wasn't going to be enough.

Reflection

What do you need help with?

In what area of your life do you sense the need for God to carry you?

Have you ever felt the absence of his presence (silence doesn't mean absence)?

16

One Decision Away from Stupid

I was inspired by a particular story that took place years ago. It's a sad story, a devastating story that does not have a good ending. The person in this story really was one decision away from stupid.

I was in bed when I heard the phone ring. It was almost time for me to get up, so I answered it. My husband had already left for work at the time, so I would be hearing the news all alone. My friend was on the other line. This wasn't just any friend; she was the one who cared about current news events so much that she took it upon herself to make sure everyone on her "friend" list got a phone call about it. I often wondered if she knew that we all really did have televisions and radios. Anyway, this time her story wasn't random or insignificant, but in fact it was sad and devastating.

That definitely got my attention.

If you journey back in time with me—not too far, but into the mid-1990s—there was a woman named Susan Smith who was the mother of three boys. As the story goes, this mother, who was apparently suffering from postpartum depression, buckled her three sons into seats of her car and systematically drove the car into a lake. The boys drowned and she survived. Survived only to see that she was, in fact, on the wrong side of that decision. But it was too late. The boys would just be a memory. Some people dared say that on that day Susan Smith became the poster child of "what not to do."

Fast-forward several years, as I am parenting four children. Four children that the LORD blessed me with. The oldest got the brunt of my anger and frustration. Not only because of my unhealthy state of mind, but also because of his consistent defiance and rebellion. After years of failed discipline methods, ineffective counseling appointments and a growing apathy in my son to make good choices, we made a tough decision to register him in military school. Before we found out he had been accepted into the six-month in-house program an hour from our home, I found myself eerily close to Susan Smith's disposition with my own children. Especially my oldest. Please don't misunderstand. I wasn't going to drown my son or any of my other children. That day I became acutely aware that I was now one decision away from stupid, because I could see I was at my breaking point. Between my thought process and inability to apply self-control, I knew I was in trouble. I didn't want to live that way. Yet what I worried about was "what if I am one decision away from stupid, and I'm on the wrong side of it?"

So, the first decision we made was for our son to live away from home until he went to military school. A week turned into three and then we got the acceptance letter for him to go there. He still wasn't allowed to move back in—another difficult but good decision.

Once at military school, we began receiving letters of great hope penned with his own hand. I went from being skeptical to accepting to genuinely hopeful over the course of the next several weeks. I hadn't had that feeling of true hope in a very long time. I almost didn't recognize it. Not only was I thankful for the work God was doing in my heart, but I was really beginning to like the result of our decision.

So why is this significant? I believe every person deals with this no matter what season of life we are in. *Making decisions that will either end well or that won't.* And on what bases do we make those decisions? Are they from a foundational way of thinking? Perhaps personal bias, religion, education, or simply an educated guess? Although there have been many decisions over the years that I have been pleased with, there have been some that have been less than stellar. For starters, I'm glad I said yes to my husband when he wanted to pursue a dating relationship with me—it ended in marriage. In fact, we continue to date each other as we raise our children. Then saying yes to the three pregnancies I had resulted in three handsome young men. Saying yes to God when he called us to adopt our daughter has resulted in a tighter relationship between him and I and a growing love for a child that grew in my heart and not in my womb.

Saying no to leadership positions when I knew full well I wasn't trained or prepared in any way resulted in more time with my family and less time with my face in the dirt. Saying no to Satan's attacks in my life, while saying yes to God's power and presence continues to result in a growing faith and internal strength that some only dream of. I could go on and on about decisions I've made that ended well, some didn't and while yet others are still developing into something today and perhaps for years to come.

I'm most thankful for the decision I made to follow Christ with all my heart, soul, mind, and strength. For me, to make decisions without Christ was really lonely and lacked purpose. To make a commitment to follow Christ opened up a world full of his purpose for my life, his miraculous ways, and a host of other things that keep unfolding throughout this journey. Now, decades later, my life is full of great potential and purpose. Saying yes to Jesus has resulted in having my future sealed for his return. Life after death for me will be spent with Jesus in heaven. When it comes to my faith, I never want to be one decision away from stupid. Saying no to Jesus secures your eternity in hell.

What side of that question are you on?

If you are on the side that results in an eternity in hell, take heart; it's not too late for repentance and embracing that gift of eternal life. God is a forgiving God; he is waiting for you and his love for you stretches to the heavens and is as far as the east is from the west.

Reflection

Have you heard of Jesus and his undying love for you?

How do you handle decisions in your life?

When have you felt like you were "one decision away from stupid"?

17

Army Boots

"Your momma wears army boots."

Why would anyone say that? Why are they making fun of his momma? I would often ask myself when I heard that phrase shouted from one student to another in our high school. I think it might have been a way of showing off strength while mocking the person.

I recently found myself in a very complicated set of circumstances when that phrase came back to me, what I thought was "out of the blue." It felt so unrelated to anything I was currently facing, but I wrote it on a piece of paper anyway, wondering if God was trying to tell me something. He was. He did.

As I unpacked what the LORD was laying on my heart, it was profound and yet very simple.

Army boots are used in combat or in preparation for combat. For some, simply as a fashion statement. The pairing of army boots with a fashion-forward minidress used to stump me until I realized the visual it created. To me, it becomes the marriage of strength and femininity. Nothing wrong with that, in my opinion.

What intrigues me most about army boots is that they have a strong resemblance to a phrase I often read, "feet fitted with the readiness that comes from the gospel of peace," right out of Ephesians 6. This chapter emphasizes the battle that rages among us—the spiritual forces of evil versus God—and how we can equip ourselves for that battle. In this passage of Scripture we learn how to dress for that battle. It reminds us that the battle is "not against flesh and blood," and it helps us be prepared for it. The armor of God. When we put on our armor we choose to protect ourselves with the covering God intended for us. So the fact that he has provided us with a covering for our feet suggests his version of "army boots."

The spiritual battle for our minds and our souls began back in the garden of Eden. When Eve took the fruit, after believing a lie, and Adam stood by passively.

Through several stories in the Old and New Testaments, we hear about the results of that initial battle. The battle won't be over until Jesus returns. So we need to remain in combat mode until then and not be passive. We might be in the battle, but we need to remember Who won the war.

Getting back to the original statement—"Your momma wears army boots"—that's a phrase from a bully. The Enemy (i.e., Satan) is a bully who really plays dirty. I believe, and the Bible teaches, that he lies to us and can throw our minds into great confusion and disharmony at his whim. We need to take every thought captive to the authority of Christ. I take comfort in the fact that he has *no power* in the life of a Christ follower. The Enemy is always looking to gain ground in our lives, and we need to be proactive in not handing over to him what belongs to God.

I am a mother of four. A wife to one. I, with God's help, choose to protect those under my care. I'm a momma that wears army boots. I'm in the LORD's army! I do combat passionately with Christ at my side. He is on the throne of my life. The Enemy is his footstool. I might not wear minidresses (for several reasons), but the power of Christ in my life has definitely strengthened my femininity.

The Enemy's position is under our feet. Let's stomp him out with our army boots!

Reflection

How does spiritual warfare show up in your story?

Do you wear "army boots"? (You don't even have to be a momma!)

What piece of armor do you need on your journey right now?

In what ways has the Enemy attacked you?

18

Accept the Unexpected

(Inspired by Matthew 14–16)

During the Advent season, we are encouraged to prepare for the coming of a Prophet, Priest, and King in the form a tiny baby boy—God becoming flesh. We even sing a song with the lyrics, "Come, thou long-expected Jesus." We know what to expect, right? Maybe, maybe not. Depends where you find yourself in the salvation story.

In this season, so many unbelievers sing, "Joy to the world, *the LORD* has come." Ah, the irony of the season comes through again. We spend eleven months out of the year arguing our position and the existence, or for some, nonexistence of God. Then in the month of December, we celebrate such unity in our caroling and gift giving . . . just as the "three wise men and the shepherds did." (Side note: Scripture isn't clear on whether there were three wise men or more; I am making reference to how this has been described over the generations.) Are you expecting the Savior in a manger? Or just a baby in a straw bed with a bunch of animals, shepherds, and wise men bringing gifts? *Who* are you expecting? Will you accept the unexpected this Christmas?

Okay, try if you can to put the hustle and bustle of the season behind you for just a moment. What has dropped into your life unexpectedly? Are you accepting it?

Maybe it's a recent diagnosis of an illness or the breaking of a relationship. Perhaps it's the loss of a job or the death of a loved one. The list could go on. Were you expecting one or more of those things to happen? I imagine it's still hard to accept whether you were expecting it or not.

When the unexpected is negative, it's harder to accept. I believe that's when we enter a valley on our journey. I recently wrote a post about mountaintops, appropriately titled "Mountaintops." I find it interesting that in the midst of writing about mountaintop experiences, the Holy Spirit gave me the inspiration to write about valleys. Personally, I'm not a fan of life in the valley. (I haven't met too many others who are either. I'm thankful for their company.)

Wouldn't you know it, the minute I was inspired to write on this, example after example (actually more like practical ways I would have to apply the same theory to my life) came my way.

Let me share some ways in which the inspired title has played out in my life recently.

Over the past few years, my husband and I found ourselves in a particular valley surrounding parenting. We haven't always handled parenting our four precocious children in a united fashion. But in the end, we do our best to remain united and have since come out stronger than ever. During one such time, I assumed "all people who call themselves Christians" would respond with love, support, prayer, and encouragement. Not only did I miss the mark on that one, but I was once again schooled by the spelling of the word "ass-u-me." Our valley experience showed us who the "real" followers of Christ were. I found myself needing to accept the unexpected, as I surrendered my fear, rejection, sadness, and eventually my grief during that time. I asked God to show me what fruit I was looking for that would help me in my valley. The Holy Spirit inspired me with the phrase "truth-tellers and Jesus-lovers." These are people who love Jesus and live free in his truth and as a result share his truth with us. Unfortunately, not all Christians carry the quality of truth-telling. There are times that I have been deeply and truthfully encouraged by unbelievers who chose to keep it real and speak the truth. There's a verse I love that says, "They will know you are Christians by the fruit in your life" (Matthew 7:16–20; paraphrased). It doesn't matter how many verses you have memorized; if the fruit of those verses aren't showing up in your life, then they are just knowledge. Even Satan knew the Bible and misrepresented it to Eve, and he tries to do the same in our lives today.

So I did just that—I chose to accept the unexpected emotions that came along in my time in the valley. I chose to accept the unexpected condemnation about making certain decisions we made. I chose to accept the expected Word of God in Romans 8:1 that says, "Therefore, there is now *no* condemnation for those who are *in* Christ Jesus" (italics mine).

We still struggle through some of those situations, but our family is stronger because we chose to stand on the Word of God and lean into him throughout the journey.

I don't always accept the unexpected, right away, as I would like. But when I take a second to put some space between myself and the situation, I gain a better perspective. I see the space as a place where the Holy Spirit can slide a Scripture in, allowing any impatience or anxiety to shake loose. I also see that space as a "margin" in my life. I've come to learn that if everything in my life was one-thing-after-the-next, there would be no margin to catch my breath. The older I get, the more I realize that sometimes God allows the unexpected to show up in my life to give me what I need—a margin, rest, additional prayer time, an opportunity to think outside of myself, or simply a more concentrated time to be with Jesus. I'm thankful I serve a God to whom nothing is unexpected! It gives me comfort knowing, nothing touches my life without going through his fingers first.

My ability to accept the unexpected has grown in times when I have acknowledged negative feelings and surrendered them to God.

Wherever you find yourself on your journey, know that God is expectantly waiting to share that experience *with* you. Be sure to share with someone close to you so God can affirm that you are not alone.

Whether you know him personally or not, he wants you to know you are worse off than you know, and more importantly, you are more deeply loved than you think!

Will you make today the day that you accept Jesus as Prophet, Priest, and King in the midst of your unexpected moment? He's waiting for you to ask.

Reflection

Are you in a place on your journey where you are being challenged to accept the unexpected? How's it going?

What negative feelings are you currently having about a situation in your life?

19

Blowin' Smoke or Givin' Hope?

As my husband and I sat over a hefty plate of chips and salsa, we debriefed an intense counseling appointment from earlier that day. The appointment itself wasn't intense; it was the subject matter that required more brainpower than we could muster up. Thus the need for time alone together before the day was done.

We are the parents to four future adults, and we have a very major decision in front of us regarding one of them.

We have a plan A and a plan B. Both require wisdom, discernment, and prayer. We have great counsel from a professional and we have great counsel from God! God is using the words and actions of a Bible character, Ezra, combined with those of a learned man, Neil Anderson, to impact my character as we choose to step forward in this decision for our son. We are being challenged to surrender the plans for our son into the hands of God. We are being encouraged to keep our eyes on God and to avoid controlling and/or manipulating circumstances surrounding us.

Back to our salsa date. As I dipped into the hot sauce, we reminisced about all the challenges in the past with this child. We also remembered the people that spoke into our lives. Sadly, we concluded, most of the people who spoke into our life during those early years were "blowin' smoke." They were not "givin' hope." (Thus the inspiration for the title that my husband came up with.) So many well-meaning parents told us, "Your son will be okay, don't worry." Or "he'll grow out of it; he's just a kid." Or my favorite: "Boys will be boys."

Even though those phrases were fixing a short-term anxiety, I couldn't help but wonder, "How do they know?" That question quickly turned into, "But what if our son won't grow out of it?" and a whole host of other questions and wonderings.

As the years went by, the well-intentioned were sometimes also the ones that stood by and judged and criticized us. Looking back, I can count on one hand the people who spoke God's truth into our lives as they lived it out in their own. They were giving us hope. An eternal hope. One that is carrying us today. Oddly enough, those who we felt were blowin' smoke are not in our lives anymore. When the going got tougher for us, they left. The ones who poured into us a hope in Christ and his power and plan for *all* of us stayed, prayed, loved us, and encouraged us through those times.

They serve a faithful God *with* us, and it is very obvious.

I have learned, in some areas, and am continuing to learn in others, the hope of Christ in the midst of a challenging situation. Not to minimize that person's experience and not to disregard mine. That's part of God's plan for my life. It doesn't make a decision any easier, I can attest to that. It just puts my focus on Jesus and the cross rather than my challenging situation.

Perhaps you are someone that has been blessed with eternal lessons that could bless another. Blowin' smoke or givin' hope . . . I'm ready to pass the baton. Are you?

Reflection

How might God be calling you to share the hope you have found so you can be engaged in passing the baton of hope to the next generation or someone else in your life?

What are you currently facing for which you need an extra measure of hope?

Where do you find hope?

Part 3

God Sees Us

20

The Light at the Lake House

As I sat in the front room overlooking the undisturbed lake, the sun was almost one with the horizon. The lamp was on in the front window, and as I looked just behind it, I saw a swarm of moths and mosquitos (night creatures) clamoring at the glass that was actually a barrier to keep them from the light. They were drawn to the light so fiercely. For a minute I wondered if they knew the glass was in the way? But then it dawned on me that perhaps they were content to just be anywhere near the light. Please know that I'm not debating the intelligence of these creatures; I'm really just drawing a parallel that perhaps will gradually become clear. I was amazed at the reckless abandon the bugs were showing in their quest. This whole picture shed light on another (no pun intended).

Among the many names that Jesus has used to describe himself, the Light of the World seems fitting to this analogy. Jesus Christ is the Light of the World. Unfortunately, not everyone sees him that way. Those that follow him are called Christians or Christ followers. We are drawn to him in many ways—through his Word (the Bible), through worship, through the actions of other Christ followers that plant seeds and set godly examples in our life, and through a myriad of other ways. Let me be clear, though. There is only One way to God, and that is through his Son, Jesus Christ, the Light of the World. For us to be in an intimate relationship with Jesus Christ, we need to acknowledge sin—the barrier between us and God. This can be illustrated in our analogy of the bugs behind the window who didn't have a solution. They had to accept the fact that the window would not be opened to allow them access to the light.

For us, there is a solution that allows us access to the Light of the World, Jesus Christ. He gave his life as a living sacrifice on the cross, so we wouldn't have to. He tore the curtain in two so we would have free access to him. By confessing the sin in our life we clear the path to the cross. He awaits with open arms to pour out his forgiveness in abundance. He deeply desires intimacy with us. Unfortunately, some believers are content to just remain in the outer limits of his presence. Not willing to acknowledge or deal with the sin in our lives. That night, the warm glow of the lamp reminded me of the warm glow I experience in the presence of Jesus.

The local church, no matter your experience, is full of people who love him and seek to follow him in a genuine and honest way. However, there are also many who choose to live in the outer limits. It isn't about "arriving"; it's about the journey, the daily life of a believer, and a heart surrendered to the work of the Holy Spirit that propels us into an intimate relationship with Jesus.

Reflection

Are you in the outer limits? Or on the inside looking out?

Do you desire an intimate, growing relationship with Jesus?

Is there someone in your life that is pointing you to the cross?

What draws you to the community of faith you belong to?

21

Weathering the Storms

So for the past few weeks I found myself in the midst of several challenging storms. Some of them were short-lived, while others haven't ended yet, so I don't know how they will turn out.

As I prayed about how I was going to "set the stage" for a recent women's gathering our church was hosting, I also sought godly counsel about how much to share. During one of my prayer times, I heard the Holy Spirit tell me, *"Storms are messy and the outcome is not always clear."* So often we share about God's faithfulness in the context of "it's over." "God was faithful." With a nice tight bow on the answered prayers and the end of the storm. I have been led to share about God's faithfulness in the midst of the storm. Because the reality is we *all* have unfinished storms in our lives, with no tight bows on the horizon. To be honest, I'm not sure I would want the bows if it meant I didn't have Jesus.

During these past weeks, the shrill voice of the Enemy has been an icy cold breeze that has been way too familiar for me. Especially in those moments when I was doubting decisions, feeling alone, or fighting off those that were throwing stones of judgment and criticism. I just wanted to scream at all of them, "You just don't understand!"

Don't worry, I refrained. At least with my mouth.

As most of my close friends know, I'm an out loud processor. That is a very small part of why I'm sharing this. At the end of the day, if God and my husband are not on board with affirming my desire/choice to process out loud, then I will not share publicly.

So out of respect for them both, my love for the truth and a need to share, I will share this.

In the midst of the storms, *God was faithful*. I saw him. I heard him. I walked with him. I felt his hand in mine. I knew he was catching my tears. There were a lot of them too! They were so unpredictable during these storms that I didn't know when the waterworks were going to gush. (If you know me personally, you know that I don't cry a whole lot, so this was all a little foreign for me.)

There were moments I could hear God sing over me. I believe it was as a covering, a blessing, and a love gift just for me. His provision was available for my taking. The Bible says so. Don't take my word for it, look it up!

My job was to acknowledge from my heart that "he alone is God and has complete authority in my life. Nothing touches my life without going through his fingers first." I had learned that years ago and was now called to inhale that truth to the deepest parts of my soul.

He showed me a picture of my situation. I closed my eyes and saw the storms swirling around me. I was standing in the middle of a tube made of light. I knew that if I put my hand out to one side or the other, I would be swept up into all the chaos. If I took one step forward or fell back, I was a goner.

But God was *not* going to let that happen. How did I know that? Because of all the "bows" I have seen over the years. He was faithful then and He would be faithful now. He is the ultimate promise keeper.

About the storms that don't yet have an ending. They are surrendered, and I am trusting God for the outcome. I believe that he will be faithful! He will show up according to his timing and choosing. He hears my cry and catches every tear that falls. He sees me and knows me and will be faithful to complete what he began in me . . . and he will do the same for you.

Reflection

What storms or challenges are you facing in your life right now?

Are you wondering where God is in the midst of your struggles?

Take a minute and reflect on the finished and unfinished "bows" in your story.

Who do you need to forgive in the midst of these storms?

22

Let Freedom Ring

(Inspired During a Trip to Nepal)

On a recent trip to Nepal as a speaker for a first-ever women's conference, I made some startling connections to the Christian faith. One in particular that resonates deep in my soul was realized when we were visiting one of the villages in the western region of Nepal. Even though a person has been freed from physical slavery, it doesn't mean they know how to live it out. They need to be taught. They need to relearn how to live in a new and free way. But who will tell them? Who will teach them? While in the country, we primarily served the Tharu people, a group of people who have lived as indentured slaves for several generations. In the mid to late 1990s that type of slavery came to an end. Then in the early 2000s it was considered illegal to continue that kind of practice. The ministry we served alongside has bought and freed slaves since 1996. From our understanding, they have bought and freed ninety-two families. They brought the gospel of Jesus Christ to them and watched as God's hand transformed the lives and hearts of many, young and old. As a result, they began churches throughout the eastern and western regions of Nepal that are led by pastors that were trained by the ministry.

For me personally, I don't know if it was hearing about people being freed from slavery, many coming into relationships with Christ in such a short time, or the fact that thirty-six churches were formed in the past fifteen years or so, but my heart was overwhelmed. They all displayed that the hand of God had prevailed in a country that was labeled as the first Hindu kingdom in the world.

With the ending of slavery, the Tharu people also changed their name. They were no longer to be referred to as Tharu but as Rana or Chowdry. Those were new tribal names that were given to signify that the old had gone and the new had come. Also, when the practice of indentured slavery for the Tharu people had ended legally, the government gifted the said slaves with 18,000 square feet of land. To many the gift was appreciated and well received. Perhaps with some skepticism attached. As generous as the gift seemed, there were some problems—major problems. The land wasn't farmable and there was no drinking water on the premises. The ministry had helped pipe in water to some of the houses, in which case neighbors would have to share with one another, and they did.

What was even more remarkable is that many of the "freed" people built their small huts on one corner of the property. With all that land available, they were living as though they were still enslaved and were only "allowed" to use a certain space for living. That was extremely disheartening to me. I didn't understand why they would choose to do that. It was explained to me that although they were physically set free, their hearts and minds were still living as though enslaved.

Before I knew it, tears were streaming down my face. I saw, with my mind's eye, faces of brothers and sisters in Christ who were living with the same mind-set. They have been redeemed by the blood of Christ—set free—but are still living as though they are enslaved. Oh, how my heart ached. It brought me full circle to the day I closed my hair salon of fifteen years. Knowing I was experiencing the abundant life as a Christian and wanting, deeply desiring, the same for others who called themselves Christians—people who call themselves followers of Christ while their hands are firmly gripping the things of their past and the idols in their present, all the while hoping for the abundant life God promises and wondering why they aren't experiencing it. In that moment, I was also reminded of a prayer I have prayed many times over the years: *"Lord, please break my heart with what breaks yours. In Jesus' name, Amen."*

My heart breaks for people who are spiritually and emotionally enslaved, when they don't have to be. Christ went to the cross on my—our—behalf. He paid that price once and for all. He came to give life and give it abundantly while the Enemy comes to steal, kill, and destroy (John 10:10). Yet some hands are still too full to receive that incredible gift of salvation, of freedom in Christ.

That day my heart was breaking all over again. I wondered in my heart, "LORD, why don't they understand? Why don't they obey? Why aren't they following you with all their heart, soul, mind, and strength?" I can only imagine how God's heart breaks when one of his children, although redeemed, is still clutching on to the stuff that keeps them from an uninhibited relationship with Jesus Christ.

We often use the phrase "strength in numbers." Well, I wonder if we had a growing number of believers being set free from the things that keep them enslaved, how that would impact our relationships, our families, our communities, our nation, the world. Speaking to the tribal Rana and Chowdry women was a privilege and an honor. They are first-generation Christian women. Our team went there because the LORD was showing us that he was indeed expanding our territory. Now that we are home, we are tempted by the pressures in our lives to stay in our little corners. I won't. I can't.

Reflection

Where in your story do you desire spiritual freedom?

Who or what is keeping you from experiencing the abundant life?

What does freedom mean to you?

May you learn how to live your life with your hands free and heart open.

23

The Tree

Remember that song we used to sing in Sunday school (if you went to one)?

"Zacchaeus was a wee little man, and a wee little man was he. He climbed up in a sycamore tree for the LORD he wanted to see. And as the Savior passed that way he looked up in that tree. And he said, 'Zacchaeus, you come down, for I'm going to your house today.'"

Well, it's based on a story from Luke 19. It's a simple and yet profound story all at the same time. Simple because it's about a tax collector from that day. A short, little man who simply wanted to get a better view of the Savior. Zacchaeus knew him to be someone important and influential and didn't want to miss seeing him pass by. A few years ago, I heard a sermon based on that story and the challenge was presented. "What tree do you need to climb so you can get a better view of Jesus?" That is the profound part.

You see, I know that Jesus is important and I never want to lose sight of him in my life. I guess you might say I want a front-row seat whenever he is present. I know he will never leave me and he walks with me faithfully. However, I sometimes can't see him very well. Too many things in the way, too many distractions, etc. So sometimes I need to strain my neck and stand on my tippy toes . . . in other words, "climb a tree." Not only am I, like Zacchaeus, short, but I am a sinner in need of a Savior. Knowing that I'm saved by grace wasn't helping much during a time when I was struggling. I really needed to *see* Jesus. I needed a clear view of his hand. It was as if I needed to feel so close that I could touch the hem of his robe.

As a mother of four, I faced a lot of challenges when the kids were little. As our oldest prepares to enter adulthood, things have gotten even more challenging . . . or so it seems. It doesn't help that the oldest is taller than I am. (At least Zacchaeus had a tree to climb. I often find myself looking for my own tree during those difficult exchanges.) Although surrendered, I have been known to carry some regret from the early years of parenting him. I need to *see* Jesus.

But God is a God of second chances, right? Well, he has given me a second chance—our adopted daughter who is half his age, exactly. She comes well equipped with a very strong will; the strength of Samson in her mind and heart, it seems. I get to apply all that I learned from the challenges that came from the early years of parenting strong-willed children (assuming I learned some things). Sounds easy, right? Except that she also comes with hormonal challenges that are blooming a little early for my liking. A double whammy, if you ask me. As I'm learning, however, just because I'm teaching what I've learned, it doesn't necessarily follow that I am someone she wants to learn from. I need to *see* Jesus.

This morning in my devotions I happened to be reading Luke 19 again. Coincidence? Not so much. It's God showing me what I was going to need to do today . . . "climb a tree." So I took the first step and asked God to show me where the tree was . . . what it looked like so I wouldn't miss it. So I could *see* Jesus in full view! I needed clarity and a new perspective. I needed to *see* Jesus.

Little did I realize that by asking God for his help I was already climbing a tree . . . the cross. His tree. One that is secure and will hold me no matter what. After all, my sin is already hanging on it. Maybe that's why the challenges I faced with my daughter on this day were uncovering some pain in my heart from situations of the past. I felt prickly. I was remembering my failures when I was raising my firstborn at that age. I was remembering the growing frustration with his failures and struggles and that I couldn't do anything about them then, or now. I needed to feel the blood of Christ soothing my wounds from the past years of parenting as I clung to that tree. I needed to hear him call my name and tell me I was okay. I needed to *see* Jesus.

I climbed the tree. I saw Jesus. He saw me, called my name, and reminded me Whose I am. That I have been redeemed. That I am not the mom I used to be. Even though I didn't think to seek Jesus when I first became a mom, I am so grateful for his grace that covered my mistakes, filled in the gaps. I have grown to appreciate less of me and receive more of him. As difficult as it is to parent someone else's biological child, I knew I couldn't do it without the permanent presence of God in my life. I find comfort in the fact that he created her. He knows what she needs. He knows how she is wired. He even saw that I was the right mother for her as he chose us to be her forever family. When I question that, he reminds me that when she joined our family I prayed God would always show me his thumbprint in our story. I guess he's doing just that. He did that by changing my heart, changing the direction my heart was facing. Instead of facing my own abilities, he has taught me to face him . . . through thick and thin. He has also taught me to stay honest and real about this adventure of parenting. I'm not a perfect parent, and I've never claimed to be. There is only one perfect parent and that is Jesus Christ. Today I *saw* Jesus. He *saw* me. He came to my house. How about you?

Reflection

What "tree" do you need to climb?

Which way are you facing?

Have you asked him to come to your house?

Are you sensing him inviting himself into your story?

Where are you seeing his thumbprint in your life?

24

Stay in Your Lane

I love writing. Years ago if you would have asked me if I did, the answer would have probably been no. But now, decades after graduating from college, I reflect on the experiences the LORD has given me and I find great inspiration to write about them. From friendships to marriage to parenting to ministry, there has been so much to learn about and so much to write about, as the LORD leads.

To use a driving / car racing analogy, in my life the Holy Spirit has been the "pace" car. I haven't always followed his lead very well. In fact, during my young adult years, I would go ahead of him and then reap the consequences of my actions. I would lose my direction, allowing fear and anxiety to set in. I learned that life is not a circle (like a track) where we are free to go ahead of the "pace" car and still successfully arrive at the finish line. The track of life is open-ended. I learned through my struggles of competition, misappropriated anger, disappointments, health issues, difficult children etc., that I needed a pace car. I needed Jesus.

What locked it in for me was a prayer that my pastor taught us at church. Not only did he share it with us, he was living it as well. The prayer was this: "*LORD, help me to listen to and obey the promptings of the Holy Spirit.*" I wrote it on a 3x5 card and put it on my nightstand so I would see it as the last thing at night and the first thing in the morning. Over time, by the work of the Holy Spirit in my life, I surrendered.

I could see a change in my heart, my choices, my pace, my desires, and my longings. More importantly, my husband and those close to me saw a change and a growth in me. I wanted what God wanted for me; I chose to go at his pace. I longed for my heart to break with the same things that broke his heart. I longed to serve him with all of me. My desires became about him and not about me. I learned how to get out of the way and let him lead. I have a ways to go, but these days my response to his leading is much quicker.

We have so many choices in life. So many "lanes" to travel in. But God calls us to live in the lane that is specific for each of us. Some would refer to it as "our calling." My calling is my responsibility. Your calling is yours. I can't enter your lane until you have given me permission. You can't enter into mine for the same reason. You can't tell me how to parent my children; you can only encourage me on the journey. Don't get me wrong, suggestions are great, when invited. I can't tell you how to lead your ministry if you are the worship leader; I am not.

The Bible teaches about "walking with one another." We need to do that. It doesn't tell us to go around telling people what to do. By now you might be saying, "You are telling us what to do!"

Yes, because by choosing to read this book you have invited me into your journey.

Since we each have our own lane or calling, whichever you would prefer to use, God wants to join us in that lane. God has called you to something. Jesus wants to be your "pace" car, your guide and example. He gives us the Holy Spirit as our companion for the journey.

Just as I have been hoping you would join me on this journey of my love for writing, he is waiting for you to invite him into your lane.

Your life is your race, not someone else's.

Stay in *your* lane. Be *your*self in the journey. Keep *your*self connected to Jesus!

Reflection

How will you choose to continue and finish the race set before you?

What does your lane look like?

Where and/or what is the pace car on your road?

25

Feet in His Palm

A few weeks ago, good friends of ours returned from a year-and-a-half adventure in Cameroon, West Africa. As I imagined what they were going through trying to reestablish themselves back in the American culture, I realized that their dependence on God was definitely going to be tested.

Before they left to serve overseas, they rented out their house, and sold vehicles, and rented storage units for their personal remaining belongings. Even though the parents answered God's call to serve overseas, they committed themselves as a family for this great undertaking. To me that showed great courage and a strong commitment to a faithful God.

Shortly after they had returned from almost two years away, I was over at their house and we conversed about the transition and the need for jobs, along with discernment to make the right decisions. I commented with, "So you all are really trying to figure out how your feet fit back on the palm." We all stopped and remarked about the power of that statement. For those who don't know, Michigan is shaped like a hand—the mitten state, as it is called. If you've ever spoken to a local resident, they will often use their hand to show you where their city is located in reference to the mitt. Since I didn't grow up here, it's taken me years to figure out which hand describes it best, and I've decided that for me it's my right hand. That exposes the palm.

As followers of Christ, we often refer to our lives as "in God's hands." This conversation connected me with my spiritual journey with Jesus. It made me wonder about the ways by which God's (palm) hand has been exposed in my life. What are the things that draw me to his hand? Are they broken relationships? My health? The health of my husband or children? Rejection, disappointment, hurt, judgment, loss? Perhaps it's simply my brokenness, in general, that draws me to him. There are many things that pull us away from him. In fact, I'll bet if you took out a scrap paper and began writing the things that pull you away from an intimate, comforting relationship with Jesus, you could fill a page in minutes. From painful memories of your childhood to the (only sometimes perceived) responsibilities of today.

I'd like to share another story with you. Over the course of the past fifteen years, I have had five foot surgeries. As a result, I have weak bones in my feet. So recently, I developed a foot fracture that caused me to not-so-graciously walk around in a boot (i.e., flat surgical shoe). The comfort was that since it was a black boot, it matched pretty much any outfit I had on during the healing process. Yes, I went there. However, I soon found out that I was more comfortable wearing sweats every day and didn't "feel" like dressing up. And yes, all my sweatpants are black.

In all seriousness, how I was feeling on the inside was showing up on the outside. There was nothing I could do with the stress fracture, besides wear the boot. I think those feelings of inadequacy began to spill over into how I saw myself. No matter what, people were going to see the boot anyway. I thought that "being more relaxed in how I dressed" would somehow give people the message that I was "resting" and taking care of myself, allowing my foot to heal faster somehow.

During this time I was also seeing a physical therapist for lower back pain, which was aggravated by the imbalance in my feet from having to wear the flat surgical shoe. Then it happened . . . the all-too-familiar (and sometimes annoying) phrase came to me—"No pain, no gain." What does that have to do with anything right now? I'm not exercising (as I need or even want to), so there is none of that kind of pain. In fact, I'm feeling as though during this "pain" cycle all I'm doing is *gaining weight!* Not cool. So I pray and ask God to clarify for me the timing of this statement. I also ask him what he is trying to teach me during this *painful* season in my life. Then I chuckle in the privacy of my van, because I've had this back pain for four months and the stress fracture for three weeks. Apparently I haven't learned whatever lesson I need to. By the way, as I write this, the stress fracture has healed; the boot is off! The back pain, however, seems to be getting more intense. I'm realizing that whatever he is about to "clarify" for me about lessons to be learned might actually get harder. He's not done with me yet (on so many levels).

Wait for it, wait for it . . . "If you don't experience *pain*, you will not *gain* what I want to teach you."

This constant pain is drawing me to the comforting hand of my God. God has been using this *pain* to draw me to himself. I have *gained* much . . . let me share with you a few things that I've learned during this time of agony.

1. I actually enjoy reading longer passages of Scripture, especially when I have to sit with an ice pack against my back.

2. I like to sit and write. (I have had more time to write what God has laid on my heart.)

3. I need to take the opportunity to remember one of my personal favorite phrases: "Nothing touches my life without going through his fingers first."

4. I like to eat (usually carbohydrates) when I can't exercise the way I like to . . . thus the weight gain. Probably taking on a "Who really cares?" attitude.

5. I need to learn to balance my physical, spiritual, and emotional needs.

How do you respond to pain in your life? A tattoo and piercing artist friend of mine, when asked, said that some of her clients have released their bladders during a session. Now that's a response to pain. A messy one at that. But I know you can relate, because you've probably had some very "messy" responses to your painful situation. God hears each cry and catches every tear that falls. Make today that day that you take a step closer to him. Closer to his hand. He will not disappoint.

Here are some verses to help you get a jump start to getting closer to his hand: Proverbs 3:5–6; Isaiah 52; Jeremiah 29:11–13; Matthew 6:33–34; John 15:5; Romans 8:1, 15–28; 1 John 1:9.

If we are followers of Christ, then we are already in his hand. If we aren't currently following him with our lives, but were baptized, then we were *placed* in his hand.

I don't know if you are someone who confidently acknowledges your place in God's hand, or someone who can't even see the shadow of his hand in your life. Be assured, that God knows and is still very present whether you "feel" him or not. Even though in his Word God promises, "He will never leave you nor forsake you," I know that some people still walk around "feeling" abandoned. Perhaps it's time to look at your position in relation God's hand. Are you in it? He has a big hand and there is plenty of room on it for all of us.

Reflection

Are you trusting your life to your own hands or God's?

How are you showing that you are surrendered in your heart?

26

The Claw, II

This analogy about forgiveness bears repeating.

Unforgiveness in our heart is like a claw with a chain. The claw pierces our heart and wraps itself around it, and the chain extends all the way to another person whom we are unwilling to forgive. The piercing sometimes leads to a suffocating and debilitating feeling. As we choose to forgive the other person before the LORD, then he is the one who fills our heart with love and compassion for the other person and expands it. As our heart expands, the claw loses its grip and pops off. As a result, when true forgiveness happens, you become separated from the chain that binds you to that person.

I often find myself in a place where my heart hurts. I can feel the points of the claw piercing my tender heart. Why should my heart be tender? Because I am a person that believes in Jesus and have received his forgiveness that he poured out for my sin (Matthew 26:28; Luke 22:20).

Today, I'm there again, facing the ugly sin of racism. You'd think that as a woman well into my forties, this issue wouldn't bother me as much anymore. But it does. It bothers me deeply because it is something that breaks God's heart every time it happens.

Take a walk in my shoes for a minute won't you . . . I was born in India, grew up in Canada and now live in the USA with my Dutch-American husband and four biracial children.

In my growing-up years, I have had eggs thrown at me while three young boys yelled racial slurs. My ears have been pierced with mocking laughter that has gone deep into my soul. I have been sized up walking into a retail store and asked for two pieces of identification as "store policy." I have been ignored in restaurants when out on a date with my husband. I mean, come on, if you want to know "What would she like for dinner?" then ask me, not my husband. Don't even ask me to talk about lack of eye contact or the questions about why my last name doesn't match my first name or skin color. Best one yet, "Is that your real skin color?" Ugh!

Before you think I am writing this to rant, I am not. Racism is real and unfortunately very alive because it is being fueled by the Enemy to tear down people groups. It is a sin. If you are a follower of Christ, then you also have a role to play—stand up against it. Either you will be part of the problem, or become part of the solution. As an adult, my experiences with racism continued. However, I would need to face them with the maturity that comes with age.

Years ago, while I was babysitting a friend's five-year-old, the little girl asked me the question, "Why do you have dirty skin?" Realizing her innocence and imagination as a five-year-old, I gave her a free pass and told her my skin wasn't dirty, just darker than hers because God made me this way. "So you are never going to be white?"

"No, I'm not," I replied. She replied with, "Oh, that's too bad." I was speechless. I wasn't going to get into it with a five-year-old. It left me wondering where and how she landed on that conclusion.

Then there's the marriage issue. I am in an interracial marriage. For those who have made comments like, "That must be hard," I say, "Yup, two sinful beings and one with a better tan!" (What can I say? My husband is competitive.) In our early married years, my husband and I served in ministry to teenagers together. He was the youth pastor and I was active as a small group leader. As we often did, we would take time to discuss heavy topics so as to help stretch the minds of these young people. Well, one day I decided to bring up the subject of interracial dating. I wasn't ready for what came next. One student said, "Not cool," while another one said, "Our parents would disown us, for sure, if we brought someone home who wasn't Dutch or white." After I found my pulse again and calmed my gut from wanting to throw up, I asked them if they knew Ken and I were in fact in an interracial marriage, just in case that wasn't clear. To that they said, "We don't see you as a different color. We see you as white like us."

There began my journey of discovering how the sin of racism was taking its toll on me. Internally, I was screaming, yelling, and throwing fits about the presence of racism in the church. I vented in my journal, to my husband, to my close friends (some of whom I lost because they couldn't handle the painful reality of what I was experiencing). Finally, at the cross. I brought it all to Jesus. I confessed my anger, my growing resentment, my pain. I cried out in my pain, my hurt, and for the rejection of something that will never change . . . my skin color.

So, back to the original title and its inspiration—the claw of unforgiveness.

After confessing all I was feeling so I wouldn't be tempted to sin in my anger (Ephesians 4:26), the Holy Spirit drew my attention to the growing unforgiveness in my heart. The claw had pierced my heart. It was painful! With his help, I was able to forgive all the above-mentioned situations and people involved. I didn't want the claw to destroy my life or my witness for Jesus.

With God's help, the unforgiveness was turned into surrender. You see, at the cross is where it began. The cross is where "*it* is finished" (John 19:30, italics mine).

Racism won't go away until Jesus returns. It isn't finished with its destruction. In fact, so far this year alone, two very public situations related to my race have caused the racists in this country to trash talk their way to the masses. One of those situations occurred just today. I saw the claw on the horizon, wiggling its way toward my heart so as to trap me with the growing anger in my heart. Today, I chose forgiveness.

Reflection

In what situations do you find it hard to forgive someone?

How does the sin of racism impact your story?

As far as racism is concerned, are you part of the problem or part of the solution?

27

Enemies

When I think of enemies, I feel nervous and anxious. Mostly because having enemies means there are people in this world that don't like me and seek to harm me. Imagine that. The reality is, I have enemies and so do you. Not necessarily the kind that will attack physically at any moment, but they linger and try to take advantage of my strength and confidence at any given moment.

While our family was enjoying a week at a friend's cottage, I had the privilege of swimming in the lake. First, let me say, although I was very thankful for a week at a cottage on a private lake, I don't like swimming in lakes. I prefer pools. I feel safer swimming in a pool. When in a lake, I often wonder if there will be something hanging on me when I get out. (Too many experiences with leeches, I guess.) While at home, I swim regularly to stay in shape. Second, I gave myself the challenge to swim laps to keep up with my "at-home" routine, and if you know me personally, you know I can't give up a good challenge. I went through some mental exercises to prepare myself (i.e., convince myself it was good for my health, even though it was in a lake) and then just went for it. A couple of my kids had said they'd join me in doing laps. (I think that was just their way of getting me to do it because they both backed out as soon as they saw me take the first of many strokes.)

When I completed the first lap, I was exhausted! More than usual . . . heavy breathing, feeling like my lungs were going to explode kind of exhausted. But the "fighter" (or fool) in me pushed me to doing another three laps. Yes, I'm on vacation. (Some things I just don't like to leave at home, I guess.) Four laps later I had a sense of accomplishment accompanied with great fatigue, of course. (I know it was only four, but don't judge. You didn't see how big they were!) But it felt good and I lingered in the sweet smell of success.

As I dried off and looked for a spot to soak up some sun, I began thinking about why this swim in the lake was semi-traumatizing. Then it dawned on me. There are enemies in the water with me. Seaweed, bugs, fish, other water creatures, moss; did I mention bugs? I was worried about getting bugs in my mouth or getting stuck in the long stalks of seaweed or, worse yet, a random snake or fish that might touch my skin. (Again, please don't judge. I'm a city girl, not one for the country.)

In a pool, there is only one enemy . . . me. I work hard to convince myself that swimming laps really is good for every muscle in my body . . . especially the flabby, worn-out ones. I will say that I really do enjoy the accomplishment of such a feat. But at the slightest inkling that a lane is not available, I'm in the hot tub commiserating with others about that hardship (written with undertones of sarcasm!).

All this talk about enemies gets me thinking about one very specific Enemy who is prowling around like a lion waiting for someone to devour. Some are afraid to make mention of this Enemy. To them I encourage claiming the power of God and acknowledging their position in Christ. On the other hand, some give him too much credit for the hardship in their lives instead of looking at their situation in light of the cross. Don't get me wrong, we need to give credit where credit is due. Let's be honest: our sin is a way that Satan and his fallen angels have access to our lives. We need to live with a balanced perspective. A healthy perspective of the real Enemy requires us to know and understand our position in Christ. The Bible teaches that for a follower of Christ, Satan's position is under our feet—nowhere else. I recently saw a T-shirt that read, "I wrote Satan's name on the bottom of my shoe and put my foot down!" Well put. Great visual.

As I was talking to a woman recently, I saw, in my sanctified imagination, a picture of her acknowledging her position in Christ with Satan under her feet while at the same time holding his hand, allowing him to lead her into sin. So to her I said, "Let go of his hand and keep stomping!"

The power of the cross is diminished in our lives when we give in to the power of the Enemy. When we give in to the attacks he so strategically sets off, we grow farther away from seeing the hand of God. We become convinced that if God were present, he would "rescue us." When we do that, I think we are forgetting the truth that he will *never* leave us. God *is* present in every situation. However, he won't always rescue us but will *always* make a way for us to escape. Our job is to lean into him and pay attention to his leading.

A prayer phrase I often use is, "LORD, help me to listen to and obey the promptings of the Holy Spirit." No matter my circumstances, the LORD always has a plan ready for me to discover.

Reflection

Who are the enemies in your life?

How do you respond or react when you experience an attack from the Enemy?

When was the last time you prayed for someone you thought was your enemy?

Where, in your life, is sin feeding the Enemy?